The Wilding of America

Money, Mayhem, and the
New American Dream

DANGEROUS

Kristina V. Ramos

T HE SOUND OF FOOT SHACKLES DRAGGING ON THE PAVEMENT is not a pleasant one, but neither is the feeling of them around bony ankles. Aside from foot shackles, I also have handcuffs that are connected to a chain around my waist—which is almost doubled because, apparently, they don't come in women's extra-small.

It's not easy getting on a bus in sandals and shackles, but some-how, I manage. My seat is facing the door that the officer closes behind me. Without really looking at the other passengers, I quickly realize that I am the only woman on the bus. With my peripheral vision I can tell that there are at least twenty men, probably closer to forty. All of them are wearing red jail uniforms and shackles. Millions of questions pop into my head at once. Why aren't they wearing orange? Doesn't red mean *dangerous*? Why am I on a bus full of murderers? What else could they be? Child molesters? Violent maniacs? I haven't made up my mind about

Contemporary Social Issues

George Ritzer, *Series Editor*

Urban Enclaves: Identity and Place in America
Mark Abrahamson, *University of Connecticut*

Just Revenge: Costs and Consequences of the Death Penalty
Mark Costanzo, *Claremont McKenna College*

The Wilding of America: Money, Mayhem, and the New American Dream
Charles Derber, *Boston College*

Between Politics and Reason: The Drug Legalization Debate
Erich Goode, *State University of New York, Stony Brook*

The Myth of Self-Esteem
John P. Hewitt, *University of Massachusetts, Amherst*

Contemporary Social Issues
Series Editor: George Ritzer, *University of Maryland*

The Wilding of America

Money, Mayhem, and the New American Dream

Third Edition

Charles Derber
Boston College

Worth Publishers

Acquisitions Editor: Valerie Raymond
Executive Marketing Manager: Renée Altier
Associate Managing Editor: Tracey Kuehn
Art Director, Cover Designer: Babs Reingold
Text Designer: Lissi Sigillo
Production Manager: Barbara Anne Seixas
Composition: Matrix Publishing Services
Printing and Binding: R. R. Donnelley and Sons Company
Cover photo: Richard Olsenius/National Geographic Image Collection/Getty
Images

Library of Congress Cataloging-in-Publication Number available upon request

ISBN: 0-7167-0956-2

Worth Publishers
41 Madison Avenue
New York, NY 10010
www.worthpublishers.com

To my students, past and present, who give me hope for our future

About the Author

Charles Derber is Professor of Sociology at Boston College and former director of its graduate program on Social Economy and Social Justice. He is a prolific scholar in the field of business, economy, international relations, and society, with eight internationally acclaimed books and several major research grants. Derber's most recent book, *People Before Profit: The New Globalization in an Age of Terror, Big Money, and Economic Crisis* (Picador, 2003) has been translated into Chinese, German, Arabic, and British English. His other books include *Corporation Nation* (St. Martin's, 2000), a widely discussed analysis of the growing power and responsibilities of corporations in the U.S., recently translated and published in China. His books also include *The Pursuit of Attention* (Oxford, 2000), *The Nuclear Seduction* (with William Schwartz, University of California Press) and *Power in the Highest Degree* (with William Schwartz, Oxford).

Derber espouses a public sociology that brings sociological perspectives to a general audience. Derber lectures widely at universities, companies and community groups, and appears on numerous media outlets. His op-eds and essays appear in *Newsday*, the *Boston Globe* and other newspapers, and he has been interviewed by *Newsweek, Business Week, Time* and other news magazines. He speaks frequently on National Public Radio, on talk radio, and on television. His work has been reviewed by the *New York Times*, the *Washington Post*, the *Boston Globe*, the *Boston Herald*, the *Washington Monthly*, and numerous other magazines and newspapers.

Contents

Foreword   xi
Preface   xiii
Acknowledgments   xvi

**1 The Good Man Fills His Own Stomach:
All-American Crimes and Misdemeanors   1**
Wilding in Black and White   1
The Mountain People: A Wilding Culture   5
The Ik in Us   7
Economic, Political, and Social Wilding   10
Wilding and Not Wilding: Varieties of Individualism   11
The Two Americas: Are We All Wilders?   13
Wilding and the New American Dream: Individualism
    Today and Yesterday   14
Roots of Wilding: Durkheim, Marx, and the
    Sociological Eye   17

**2 The Ultimate Wilders: Prisoners of the American
Dream   21**
Robert Oakley Marshall: "Speed Demon on the Boulevard of
    Dreams"   22
Them and Us: Violence and the Oversocialized American
    Character   26
Lyle and Erik Menendez: A Family of Competitors   28
Then and Now: An American Tragedy   33
Susan Smith: Infanticide and the Honor Student   36

3 Cheaters, Cynics, Dot-Commers, and Survivors: Wilding Culture in the Media and Everyday Life 38

Temptation and Survival: Reality TV and the Ik-ing of America 40

Downtime: A New Wilding Recipe 42

Young and Wild: Drinking, Cheating, and Other Campus Sports 44

All-American Drug Dealing: Unattainable Goals and Illegitimate Means 48

4 U.S. Business vs. Us: Global Capitalism and Corporate Wilding 51

A Fish Rots from the Head First 51

Capitalism vs. Community: Sociological Prophets and Global Profits 53

The Musical Chairs of Global Business: The New Corporate Wilding 55

Wilding around the World: The Third World as Global Sweatshop 56

Globalization without Wilding: The Future of Globalization after the Battle of Seattle 61

5 Enron: Systemic Wilding in the Corridors of Power 65

Enron and Systemic Wilding 66

Arthur Andersen: Master of Unaccountable Accounting 68

Wilding on Wall Street 69

George W. Bush and the Corporate State: Systemic Wilding in Washington, D.C. 72

6 Wilding in the Church: Unaccountable Brethren and Voices of the Faithful 76

Pedophilia, Sexual Abuse, and Rape: Wilding among the Priests 77

Cardinal Bernard Law and the Cover-up: The Church as Institutional Wilder 79

Enron, the Corporate State, and the Church: Wilding and the Collapse of Institutional Accountability 81

How to End Wilding in the Church: Empower the Laity 83

7 Killing Society: The Ungluing of America 86

Wilding in the Streets 86

Falling Bridges, Potholes, and Peeling Schoolroom Paint: The Abandonment of Society 90

The End of Government? Compassionate Conservatives, New Democrats, and Political Wilding 92

Texan Justice: Political Wilding and the Prison-Industrial Complex 98

8 War and Wilding: Iraq and the War against Terrorism 102

War in Iraq 103

Legality 105

Justice 108

The War on Terrorism 110

9 Beyond Wilding: Resurrecting Civil Society 114

The Case for Hope 115

Rethinking the American Dream: A New Communitarianism? 118

The Social Market: Sociological Sense and Dollars and Cents 120

A New Bill of Rights? The Politics of Civil Society 125

Defending Our Lives: Getting from Here to There 128

Notes 133

Index 145

Foreword

As we move into the twenty-first century, we confront a seemingly endless array of pressing social issues: crime, urban decay, inequality, ecological threats, rampant consumerism, war, AIDS, inadequate health care, national and personal debt, and many more. Although such problems are regularly dealt with in newspapers, magazines, and trade books and on radio and television, such popular treatment has severe limitations. By examining these issues systematically through the lens of sociology, we can gain greater insight into them and be better able to deal with them. It was to this end that St. Martin's Press created this series on contemporary social issues, and Worth Publishers has chosen to continue it.

Each book in the series casts a new and distinctive light on a familiar social issue, while challenging the conventional view, which may obscure as much as it clarifies. Phenomena that seem disparate and unrelated are shown to have many commonalities and to reflect a major, but often unrecognized, trend within the larger society. Or a systematic comparative investigation demonstrates the existence of social causes or consequences that are overlooked by other types of analysis. In uncovering such realities the books in this series are much more than intellectual exercises; they have powerful practical implications for our lives and for the structure of society.

At another level, this series fills a void in book publishing. There is certainly no shortage of academic titles, but those books tend to be introductory texts for undergraduates or advanced monographs for professional scholars. Missing are broadly accessible, issue-oriented books appropriate for all students (and for general readers). The books in this series occupy that niche somewhere between popular trade books and monographs. Like trade books, they deal with important and interesting social issues, are well written, and are as jargon free as possible. However, they are more rigorous than trade books in meeting academic standards for writing and research. Although they are not textbooks, they often explore topics covered in basic textbooks and therefore are easily integrated into the curriculum of sociology and other disciplines.

Each of the books in the "Contemporary Social Issues" series is a new and distinctive piece of work. I believe that students, serious general readers, and professors will all find the books to be informative, interesting, thought provoking, and exciting.

—*George Ritzer*

Preface

More than 10 years ago, I went to New York City to talk about "wilding" on WABC, the flagship radio station of ABC. The station invited me shortly after the brutal Central Park rape of a jogger—the event that led the media to coin the term *wilding*. While I hoped to educate New Yorkers, it turned out that the Big Apple still had a few things to teach me about my subject.

As I was waiting in the studio for my turn, I heard my talk-show host, Bob Grant, talk about the city's grafitti problem and his own solution, cutting off the hands of the young offenders. I sensed I had some differences with this tough hombre, but I realized why he had invited me down. He and his callers were obsessed with the disintegration of the city and with young wilders running loose on the street.

I soon learned why, in a very personal way. The day after my conversation with Grant, I drove down at noon to a conference on the lower west side of Manhattan. After about an hour, I had a premonition that I had better check my car, this feeling probably a residue of my conversation with Grant. I walked quickly back to the street and could hardly believe my eyes. My new Honda Accord was sitting only on its naked brake drums—tires, rims, and lug nuts all stripped. In the wink of an eye, my car had been transformed into one of those abandoned vehicles one sees in deserted areas of the South Bronx, except that the windows were not broken nor the inside looted.

It was an early Saturday afternoon with a lot of people around. In a state of disbelief, I ran up to two policemen who had just arrived at the corner to write up an unrelated accident. They told me to wait, and in the next 15 minutes, I watched a parade of people drive up to my car, stop, get out, and survey my vehicle. I quickly recognized that they were interested in finishing the job: the radio, the carburetor, anything to sell.

When I pleaded with the police to help me tow the car to a garage before it was picked clean, they shrugged their shoulders and told me they could not tow it unless I had committed a crime in it. I was lucky enough to find a garage, a tow truck, and a tire shop. The shop proprietor, who told me his own car had disappeared from in front of his house in the Bronx, sounded just like Bob Grant and his callers. He wanted to know if Massachusetts, where I am from, had a death penalty. When I mentioned I was

a teacher, he said he figured kids today were becoming a generation of criminals and needed a moral education more than technical skills. As I drove off, he waved and yelled out, "Please help us raise a better generation."

His plea helped to define the mission of this book. As we move into the new century, the crises of greed and violence that motivated my desire to write this book have deepened. The most sensational news stories of the 1990s were about individual wilding by O.J. Simpson and Tonya Harding. But the most dramatic stories in the first few years of the twenty-first century have been about Enron, the Catholic Church scandal, terrorism, and America's war in Iraq. Greed and violence remain epidemic among individuals, but it is wilding by giant institutions in the economy, the government, and civil society that is now making headlines.

This has led me to publish a new edition. When wilding becomes entrenched in our most powerful institutions, it changes and debases the American Dream. Wilding becomes normalized, and the new generation is socialized to an ethos that accepts greed and violence as the path to success. Elites at the pinnacle of corporation, church, and state redefine success itself as simply money and power.

But Americans, though deluged with stories of crime and corruption, are not making the connections which would help explain the real nature of the wilding problem or what might solve it. The media continues to publicize sensational street violence and personal crimes, such as the Lacey Peterson murder and the Elizabeth Smart abduction, which sell tabloids and TV advertising. But wilding, as viewed by a sociologist, involves multiple forms of immorality perpetrated in the corporate suites as well as on the streets. Few media analysts suggest that the criminals in the corporate boardrooms and street wilders share elements of the same greed and the same dream.

Individual wilding and institutional wilding are racing out of control at the same time, reflecting new contradictions between today's American Dream and American prospects for success in an age of economic crisis and decline. Americans pursue divisive and increasingly unattainable goals, which cannot meet our deepest needs for respect, love, and justice. As the Dream beckons and recedes, the price of failure is frustration and rage; the price of success, too often, inner emptiness and debilitating fear of those left behind. Deepening inequalities, rising tides of social frustration, and corrosive moral decay threaten the bonds of community and the very survival of the social fabric.

For the citizen, this is frightening, but for the sociologist the fear is tied to a burning intellectual mission. The impending sense of social breakdown raises the question of what makes community—and society itself—possible at all. This is the core problem of sociology, one with special urgency for our highly individualistic and competitive capitalist societies, but it is not a problem for sociologists alone.

The metaphor of societal illness that the wilding epidemic evokes points to the need for all of us to become practitioners of the art of social healing. This book offers one diagnosis of our weakened but still resilient collective condition. My hope is that the illness cannot long resist an awakened community brave enough to look deeply at its shared pathologies and empowered with the insights of the sociological imagination.

Acknowledgments

I am grateful to many friends and colleagues whose excitement about this book helped it come to fruition. The enthusiasm of David Karp and John Williamson nourished my own belief in the project, and their close reading of the manuscript helped me improve the book at every stage and in every edition. Morrie Schwartz spurred me on in the original edition with his insights and always generous emotional support. I thank Noam Chomsky, Jonathan Kozol, Howard Zinn, Robert Reich, Robert Coles, Philip Slater, and Alvin Poussaint for reading the manuscript and responding to it. I am also grateful to my colleagues Mike Malec, Paul Gray, Eve Spangler, S.M. Miller, Ritchie Lowry, and Severyn Bruyn, for helpful suggestions. I thank also many former and present students, including Deb Piatelli, Jonathan White, Ted Sasson, Bill Hoynes, David Croteau, and Bill Schwartz, as well as all the other teachers, students, and readers who have let me know how valuable this book has been to them.

George Ritzer encouraged me to publish this book in the current series. Valerie Raymond, my editor in this edition, brought vision, rigor, and enthusiasm to the work, and I am very grateful to her and to all of those at Worth Publishing who have supported this book. Toni Vicari, Brenda Pepe, Maureen Eldredge, and Roberta Negrin offered indispensible office support.

I owe much to my parents, who nurtured the concern for society that animates this book. And also to Elena Kolesnikova, who heroically endured the obsessions of an author about his work. She contributed ideas, helped me overcome my doubts, and nourished me all along the way.

The Good Man Fills His Own Stomach

All-American Crimes and Misdemeanors

The readings of history and anthropology . . . give us no reason to believe that societies have built-in self preservative systems.

—Margaret Mead

Wilding in Black and White

"All day I got grabbed," said Yaneira Davis, 20, a Rutgers student. She was describing her bad Sunday, Puerto Rican Day, on June 11, 2000, in New York City's Central Park. "The attitude was," Yaneira continued, " 'I'm going to touch you, and I don't care what you say.' " Ashanna Cover and Josina Lawrence, both 21, who were also in Central Park that day, said that they were sprayed, groped, and had their tops pulled off. Stephanie, who did not want her last name used, said that 20 guys "were coming at me from all directions, and they were grabbing my butt, groping my butt, and I was screaming and I was trying to get through, trying to get away." At least 46 other women reported that groups of young men stripped them, groped their breasts and genitals, and robbed them of jewelry and purses.[1]

Videotapes captured the scene, which was then beamed around the world by satellite TV. While onlookers, including police, watched passively or with some amusement, the young victims ran in terror, trying to keep their clothes from being torn off and often screaming hysterically. The young men, many drunk or stoned, seemed to be greatly enjoying themselves, going from one woman to another and yelping with pleasure as they ogled, chased, stripped and groped their prey.[2]

The violence began during pre-festivities the night before as the young men, according to one of their lawyers, "were there chillin', smokin' a couple cigarettes and watchin' the babes go by." They escalated the violence in broad daylight and inflicted mayhem throughout the day and into the evening. Twenty men were eventually arrested. Some of the victims filed suit against police at the time for doing nothing to protect them.[3]

The graphic videotapes catapulted the event into the headlines and provoked debate everywhere about violence in America. Media pundits called the gangs of young men a "wolfpack" who felt free to commit unusually savage behavior in full public view. Journalists agreed that this was another outbreak of "wilding," reminding readers of a terrifying crime that had gripped the nation 10 years earlier. We have to return to that event if we want to understand how the term *wilding* entered our culture and became a symbol of one of America's deepest social crises.

On April 19, 1989, a group of six teenagers aged 14 to 16 went into Central Park, the very same site as the Puerto Rican Day assaults. According to police at the time, the youths came upon a young woman jogging alone past a grove of sycamore trees. Allegedly using rocks, knives, and a metal pipe, they attacked her. Some pinned her down while others beat and raped her. Police reported that one defendant, 17-year-old Kharey Wise, held the jogger's legs while a friend repeatedly cut her with a knife. They then smashed her with a rock and punched her face.[4]

What most captured public attention about the story were the spirits of the assaulters during and after their crime. According to 15-year-old Kevin Richardson, one of the boys arrested, "Everyone laughed and was leaping around." One youth was quoted by police as saying, "It was fun . . . something to do." Asked if they felt pretty good about what they had done, Richardson said "Yes." Police reported a sense of "smugness" and "no remorse" among the youths.[5]

From this event, a new word was born: wilding. According to press reports, it was the term the youths themselves used to describe their behavior—and it seemed appropriate. The savagery of the crime, which left the victim brain-damaged and in a coma for weeks, evoked the image of a predatory lion in the bush mangling its helpless prey. Equally shocking was the blasé attitude of the attackers. It had been no big deal, a source of temporary gratification and amusement. They were "mindless marauders seeking a thrill," said Judge Thomas B. Galligan of Manhattan, who sentenced three of the teenagers to a maximum term of 5 to 10 years, charging them with turning Central Park into a "torture chamber." These were youths who seemed stripped of the emotional veneer of civilized humans, creatures of a wilderness where anything goes.[6]

The story of wilding quickly became tied to the race and class of the predators and their prey. The convicted youths were black and from the inner city, although from stable working families. The victim was white, with degrees from Wellesley and Yale, and a wealthy 28-year-old investment banker at Salomon Brothers, one of the great houses of Wall Street.

To white middle-class Americans, wilding symbolized something real and terrifying about life in the United States. Things were falling apart, at least in the hearts of America's major cities. Most suburbanites did not feel their own neighborhoods had become wild, but they could not imagine walking into Central Park at night.

The fear of wilding became fear of the Other: those locked outside of the American Dream. They had not yet invaded the world most Americans felt part of, but they menaced it. The Central Park attack made the threat real, and it unleashed fear among the general population and a backlash of rage among politicians and other public figures. Mayor Koch called for the death penalty. Donald Trump took out ads in four newspapers, writing "I want to hate these murderers. . . . I want them to be afraid." Trump told Newsweek that he "had gotten hundreds and hundreds of letters of support."[7]

On December 19, 2002, in a sensational turn of events, Justice Charles J. Tejada of Manhattan's State Supreme Court took only five minutes to reverse the convictions of the five "wilders," who had already served their multi-year sentences. The judge acted after another man, Matias Reyes, in jail for murder and rape, confessed to committing the Central Park rape himself, and DNA evidence conclusively linked Reyes to the crime. It appears that the earlier confessions may have been forced in a circus trial potentially involving police misconduct and racism. Patricia Williams, a law professor who attended the 1991 trial, remembers a hysterical atmosphere in the courtroom, with tourists and celebrities "lined up around the block for admission, as though it were a Broadway show." Williams noted that the confessions were full of inconsistencies elicited by "unorthodox" police tactics. These included 18 to 30 hours "of nonstop questioning," sometimes taking place "in the back of a police car" and "in the middle of the night."[8] Twelve years later, it seemed as if the public and the police had needed to confirm their views of African-American and Latino youth—and all the "Others" in America at the time—as wilders.[9]

But while the term *wilding* may have come into the media based on a false conviction and racism, it is a surprisingly useful way to characterize an evolving and deeply disturbing feature not of African-Americans or "the

Other," but of American society as a whole. Instead of focusing mainly on the "black wilding" that did not occur in the park, suppose we think of "white wilding" as a way to characterize morally unsettling and often violent behavior that is rampant throughout our culture. As an extreme example, consider a second remarkably vicious crime that grabbed people's attention all over the country just a few months after the Central Park rape. On October 23, 1989, Charles and Carol Stuart left a birthing class at Boston's Brigham and Women's Hospital, walked to their car parked in the adjoining Mission Hill neighborhood, and got in. Within minutes, Carol Stuart, eight months pregnant, was dead, shot point-blank in the head. Her husband, a stunned nation would learn from police accounts two months later, was her assassin. He had allegedly killed her to collect hundreds of thousands of dollars in life insurance money and open a restaurant. Opening a restaurant, Americans everywhere learned, had long been Charles Stuart's American Dream.

Many white middle-class Americans seemed to believe Stuart's story when he told police that a black gunman shot him and his wife, leaving Carol Stuart dead and Stuart himself with a severe bullet wound in the abdomen. When Stuart's brother Matthew went to the police to tell them of Charles' involvement, and when Charles Stuart subsequently apparently committed suicide by jumping off the Tobin Bridge into the Mystic River, some of the threads connecting his crime to the horrible rape in Central Park began to emerge. Stuart had duped a whole nation by playing on the fear of the wild Other. Aware of the vivid images of gangs of black youths rampaging through dark city streets, Stuart brilliantly concocted a story that would resonate with white Americans' deepest anxieties. Dr. Alvin Poussaint, Harvard professor and advisor to Bill Cosby, said, "Stuart had all the ingredients. . . . [H]e gave blacks a killer image and put himself in the role of a model, an ideal Camelot type that white people could identify with."[10]

Charles Stuart's crime became a national obsession. A 21-year-old Oklahoman visiting Boston told a *Boston Globe* reporter, "You wouldn't believe the attention this is getting back home. It's all anyone can talk about. I've taken more pictures of this fur shop and Stuart's house than any of the stuff you're supposed to take pictures of in Boston."[11] The quiet Stuart block in Reading became what the *Globe* called a "macabre mecca," with hundreds of cars, full of the curious and the perplexed, parked or passing by. One reason may have been that white middle-class Americans everywhere had an uncomfortable sense that, as the nineties emerged, the Stuart case was telling them something about themselves. Stuart, after all, was living the American Dream and reaping its benefits—a tall, dark, athletic man with roots in working-class Revere, making over a hundred thousand dollars a year selling fur coats, married to a lovely, adoring wife, and living the good life in suburban Reading complete with swimming pool. Had the American Dream itself become the progenitor of a kind of wilding? Was it possible that not only the inner cities of America but its comfortable suburbs were becoming wild places? Could "white wilding" be a more serious problem than the "black wilding" publicized in the mass media and so readily embraced by the public at large? Was America at the turn of the decade becoming a wilding society?

To answer these questions, we have to look far beyond such exceptional events as the Central Park rape and the Stuart murder. We shall see that there are many less extreme forms of wilding, including a wide range of antisocial acts that are neither criminal nor physically violent. Wilding includes the ordinary as well as the extraordinary, may be profit-oriented or pleasure-seeking, and can infect corporations and governments as well as individuals of every race, class, and gender.

The Mountain People: A Wilding Culture

Between 1964 and 1967, anthropologist Colin Turnbull lived among the people of Uganda known as the Ik, an unfortunate people expelled by an uncaring government from their traditional hunting lands to extremely barren mountainous areas. In 1972, Turnbull published a haunting book about his experiences that left no doubt that a whole society can embrace wilding as a way of life.[12]

When Turnbull first came to the Ik, he met Atum, a sprightly, barefoot old man with a sweet smile, who helped guide Turnbull to remote Ik villages. Atum warned Turnbull right away that everyone would ask for food. Although many would indeed be hungry, he said, most could fend for themselves, and their pleas should not be trusted. Turnbull, Atum stressed, should on no account give them anything. But before he left that day, Atum mentioned that his own wife was severely ill and desperately needed food and medicine. On reaching his village, Atum told Turnbull his wife was too sick to come out. Later, Turnbull heard exchanges between Atum and his sick wife, and her moans of suffering. The moans were wrenching, and when Atum pleaded for help, Turnbull gave him food and some aspirin.

Some weeks later, Atum had stepped up his requests for food and medicine, saying his wife was getting sicker. Turnbull was now seriously concerned, urging Atum to get her to a hospital. Atum refused, saying "she wasn't that sick." Shortly thereafter, Atum's brother-in-law came to Turnbull and told him that Atum was selling the medicine that Turnbull had been giving him for his wife. Turnbull, not terribly surprised, said that "that was too bad for his wife." The brother-in-law, enjoying the joke enormously, finally explained that Atum's wife "had been dead for weeks," and that Atum had "buried her inside the compound so you wouldn't know." No wonder Atum had not wanted his wife to go to the hospital. Turnbull thought to himself: "She was worth far more to him dead than alive."[13]

Startling to Turnbull was not only the immense glee the brother-in-law seemed to take in the "joke" that had been inflicted on his dying sister, but the utter lack of embarrassment Atum showed when confronted with his lie. Atum shrugged it off, showing no remorse whatsoever, saying he had simply forgotten to tell Turnbull. This was one of the first of many events that made Turnbull wonder whether there was any limit to what an Ik would do to get food and money.

Some time later, Turnbull came across Lomeja, an Ik man he had met much earlier. Lomeja had been shot during an attack by neighboring tribesmen and was lying in a pool of his own blood, apparently dying from two bullet wounds in the stomach. Still alive and conscious, Lomeja looked up at Turnbull and asked for some tea. Shaken, Turnbull returned to his Land Rover and filled a big new yellow enamel mug. When he returned, Lomeja's wife was bending over her husband. She was trying to "fold him up" in the dead position although he was not yet dead, and started shrieking at Turnbull to leave Lomeja alone, saying Lomeja was already dead. Lomeja found the strength to resist his wife's premature efforts to bury him and tried to push her aside. Turnbull managed to get the cup of tea to Lomeja, who was still strong enough to reach out for it and sip it. Suddenly, Turnbull heard a loud giggle and saw Lomeja's sister, Kimat. Attracted by all the yelling, she had "seen that lovely new, bright yellow enamel mug of hot, sweet tea, had snatched it from her brother's face and made off with it, proud and joyful. She not only had the tea, she also had the mug. She drank as she ran, laughing and delighted at herself."[14]

Turnbull came to describe the Ik as "the loveless people." Each Ik valued only his or her own survival, and regarded everyone else as a competitor for food. Ik life had become a grim process of trying to find enough food to stay alive each day. The hunt consumed all of their resources, leaving virtually no reserve for feelings of any kind, nor for any moral scruples that might interfere with filling their stomachs. As Margaret Mead wrote, the Ik had become "a people who have become monstrous beyond belief." Scientist Ashley Montagu wrote that the Ik are "a people who are dying because they have abandoned their own humanity."[15]

Ik families elevated wilding to a high art. Turnbull met Adupa, a young girl of perhaps 6, who was so malnourished that her stomach was grossly distended and her legs and arms spindly. Her parents had decided she had become a liability and threw her out of their hut. Because she was too weak now to go out on long scavenging ventures, as did the other children, she would wander as far as her strength would allow, pick up scraps of bone or half-eaten berries, and then come back to her parents' place, waiting to be brought back in. Days later, her parents, tiring of her crying, finally brought her in and promised to feed her. Adupa was happy and stopped crying. The parents went out and "closed the asak behind them, so tight that weak little Adupa could never have moved it if she had tried."[16] Adupa waited for them to come back with the food they had promised, but they did not return until a whole week had passed, when they knew Adupa would be dead. Adupa's parents took her rotting remains, Turnbull writes, and threw them out "as one does the riper garbage, a good distance away." There was no burial—and no tears.[17]

Both morality and personality among the Ik were dedicated to the single all-consuming passion for self-preservation. There was simply "not room in the life of these people," Turnbull observes dryly, "for such luxuries as family and sentiment and love." Nor for any morality beyond "marangik," the new Ik concept of goodness, which means filling one's own stomach.

The Ik in Us

Long before the rape in Central Park or the Stuart murder, Ashley Montagu, commenting on Turnbull's work, wrote that "the parallel with our own society is deadly." In 1972, when Turnbull published his book, wilding had not become part of the American vocabulary, nor did most Americans yet face declining living standards, let alone the kind of starvation experienced by the Iks. Americans were obviously not killing their parents or children for money, but they dedicated themselves to self-interested pursuits with a passion not unlike that of the Ik.

In America, a land of plenty, there was the luxury of a rhetoric of morality and feelings of empathy and love. But was not the American Dream a paean to individualistic enterprise, and could not such an enterprise be conceived in some of the same unsentimental metaphors used by Turnbull about the Ik? The Ik community, he writes, "reveals itself for what it is, a conglomeration of individuals of all ages, each going his own way in search of food and water, like a plague of locusts spread over the land."[18]

America now faces a wilding epidemic that is eating at the country's social foundation and could rot it. The American case is much less advanced than the Ik's, but the disease is deeply rooted and is spreading through the political leadership, the business community, and the general population. Strong medicine can turn the situation around, but if we fail to act now, the epidemic could prove irreversible.

Only a handful of Americans are "ultimate wilders" like Charles Stuart. Such killers are noteworthy mainly because they may help wake us up to the wilding plague spreading among thousands of less extreme wilders who are not killers. Wilding includes a vast spectrum of self-centered and self-aggrandizing behavior that harms others. A wilding epidemic tears at the social fabric and threatens to unravel society itself, ultimately reflecting the erosion of the moral order and the withdrawal of feelings and commitments from others to "number one."

The wilding virus comes in radically different strains. There is *expressive wilding:* wilding for the sheer satisfaction of indulging one's own destructive impulses, the kind found among the American youth who heave rocks off highway bridges in the hope of smashing the windshields of unknown drivers passing innocently below. The hockey and soccer fathers who attack coaches and other parents are expressive wilders, as are drivers engaging in road rage. Road rage has reached such epidemic proportions— as has workplace rage, school rage, and air rage—that leading pundits now talk of "dies irae," or America's day of rage. The country's most famous perpetrator is O. J. Simpson, who acted out the domestic violence that is one of the most common and Ik-like forms of expressive wilding. His alleged repeated abuse of his wife to sate his jealousy, maintain his control, or simply gratify his emotions of the moment evokes serious questions about the nightmarish spread of family violence among rich and poor alike. The national obsession with Simpson reflects the fear that when a country's icon beats his wife black and blue, smashes her windshield with a baseball bat, stalks her, and is finally charged with her murder and acquitted in a controversial verdict, we all participate in the crime, for heroes act out the passions and values of the cultures that create them.

Although mainly an example of expressive wilding (in 2001 he was arrested for road rage violence), O. J. also modeled instrumental wilding. Not simply for fun or purely emotional gratification, *instrumental wilding* is wilding for money, career advancement, or other calculable personal gain.

Simpson began as a youngster, running with gangs and stealing food. Fantastically ambitious and opportunistic, O. J. later took naturally to a life of single-minded corporate salesmanship, obsessively remaking his voice, wardrobe, and demeanor according to the image lessons of the Hertz ad executives who greased his career. He wheeled and dealed to sign movie deals and buy companies such as the Pioneer Chicken franchise (destroyed in the L. A. riots), and eventually succumbing to the greed-soaked financial dealings that led him, along with other entrepreneurial high rollers of his era, to bad loans and collapsed business deals.

Most instrumental wilding involves garden varieties of ambition, competitiveness, careerism, and greed that advance the self at the cost of others. Expressive and instrumental wilding have in common an antisocial self-centeredness made possible by a stunning collapse of moral restraint and a chilling lack of empathy. I am mainly concerned in this book with instrumental wilding because it is the form most intimately connected with the American Dream and least understood in its poisonous effects on society.[19]

Although much wilding is criminal, there is a vast spectrum of perfectly legal wilding, exemplified by the careerist who indifferently betrays or steps on colleagues to advance up the ladder. There are forms of wilding, such as lying and cheating, that are officially discouraged, but others, like the frantic and single-minded pursuit of wealth, are cultivated by some of the country's leading corporations and financial institutions. Likewise, there are important differences in the severity of wilding behaviors; killing a spouse for money is obviously far more brutal than stealing a wallet or cheating on an exam. But there are distinct types and degrees of infection in any affliction, ranging from terminal cases such as Stuart, to intermediate cases such as the savings-and-loan crooks, to those who are either petty wilders or rarely exhibit symptoms at all. The latter categories include large numbers of Americans who may struggle internally with their wilding impulses but remain healthy enough to restrain them. The variation is similar to that in heart disease: those with only partial clogging of their arteries and no symptoms are different from those with full-blown, advanced arteriosclerosis, and those least afflicted may never develop the terminal stage of the illness. But these differences are normally of degree rather than of kind; the same underlying pathology is at work among people with mild and severe cases.

There are, nonetheless, real differences between white lies or misdemeanors (forms of petty wilding) and serious wilding of the Central Park or Charles Stuart variety. Petty wilding occurs in all cultures, will persist as long as most people are not saints, and in limited doses does not necessarily threaten civil order. When wilding is so limited that it does not constitute a grave social danger, it might better be described as "incipient wilding" and is not of concern here.

However, certain types of petty wilding are growing at an alarming rate in America, as I document in Chapter 3 in my discussion of minor lying, cheating, and ordinary competitiveness with and indifference to others. Such transgressions on an epidemic scale can reach a critical mass and become as serious a threat to society as violent crime or huge investment scams on Wall Street. It is not the degree of brutality or violence but the consequences for society that ultimately matter, and I thus consider the full spectrum of wilding acts—from petty to outrageous—that together constitute a clear and present danger to America's social fabric.

Economic, Political, and Social Wilding

Wilding, in sociological terms, extends far beyond random violence by youth gangs (the current definition in *Webster's* dictionary) to include three types of assault on society. *Economic wilding* is the morally uninhibited pursuit of money by individuals or businesses at the expense of others. *Political wilding* is the abuse of political office to benefit oneself or one's own social class, or the wielding of political authority to inflict morally unacceptable suffering on citizens at home or abroad. *Social wilding* ranges from personal or family acts of violence, such as child or spouse abuse, to collective forms of selfishness that weaken society, such as affluent suburbs turning their backs on bleeding central cities.

Economic wilders include convicted billionaire financiers Michael Milken and Marc Rich (the latter pardoned by President Clinton in 2001 after Rich's wife donated millions to the Democratic Party and Clinton's presidential library). Economic wilders are a different species from the kids in Central Park, since they wild for money rather than fun or sex. Milken was indicted on 98 counts of racketeering and jailed after confessing to six major financial crimes, while Rich escaped to Europe after being convicted of tax evasion, wire fraud, and racketeering. Partly because of differing opportunities and incentives, people wild in different ways and for exceedingly varied reasons and motives, ranging from greed and lust to gaining attention or respect. The different forms of wilding, however, are all manifestations of degraded American individualism.

Wilding is individualism run amok, and the wilding epidemic is the face of America's individualistic culture in an advanced state of disrepair.

An individualistic culture promotes the freedom of the individual and in its healthy form nurtures human development and individual rights. In its degraded form, it encourages unrestrained and sociopathic self-interest.

Wilding and Not Wilding: Varieties of Individualism

Wilding—a degenerate form of individualism—encompasses a huge variety of antisocial behavior. It includes so many seemingly unrelated acts that it might appear to stand for everything—or nothing. But wilding includes only a small subset of the entire range of behaviors that sociologists describe as individualistic, a term that arguably can be applied to any self-interested behavior. In a society such as that of the United States, dominated by individualistic values and a market system that rewards self-interest, some might argue that virtually all socially prescribed behavior has an individualistic dimension.

I propose a far more restrictive definition of wilding. Not all individualistic behavior is wilding, nor is wilding an umbrella term for any form of self-interested or "bad" behavior. As noted earlier, wilding refers to self-oriented behavior that hurts others and damages the social fabric, and this excludes many types of individualistic action. The Jewish sage Hillel wrote, "If I am not for others, what am I?" Yet he also said, "If I am not for myself, who will be for me?" His maxims suggest that many forms of self-interest are necessary and contribute to the well-being of others.

A doctor who works hard to perfect her medical skills may advance her own career, but she also saves lives. A superbly conditioned professional athlete may enrich himself by his competitiveness or ambition, but he also entertains and gives pleasure to his fans. If I strive to be the best writer I can be—an individualistic aspiration—I am educating others while fulfilling myself. In none of these cases is individualistic behavior itself necessarily wilding. Actions that advance one's own interests and either help or do not harm others are not forms of wilding, even when motivated by competitiveness or acquisitiveness.

Wilding includes only individualistic behavior that advances or indulges the self by hurting others. If the doctor advances her skills and career by cheating on tests, trampling on her colleagues, or using her patients as guinea pigs, her self-interest has degraded into wilding. The athlete who illicitly uses steroids to win competitions is wilding by cheating against his rivals and deceiving his fans.

Whereas all wilding behavior hurts others, not all hurtful behavior is wilding. If I get angry at a friend, I may hurt him, but that does not necessarily make it wilding. Such anger may be justified because it was motivated by a wrong done to me, and it may ultimately serve to repair the relation even if I am mistaken. Interpersonal relations inevitably involve misunderstanding, aggression, and hurt, which degrade into expressive wilding only when the hurt is intentional and purely self-indulgent, and when the perpetrator is indifferent to the pain inflicted on the other. Motivation, empathy, and level of harm inflicted are key criteria in deciding whether wilding has occurred. Deliberate physical or emotional abuse is clearly wilding, whereas impulsive acts that cause less harm and lead to remorse and remediation are more ambiguous cases and may not constitute wilding at all.

Similarly complex considerations apply to institutional wilding enacted by corporations or governments. Instrumental wilding takes place whenever institutions pursue goals and strategies that inflict serious harm on individuals, communities, or entire societies. Some of the most important forms of economic wilding, both legal and criminal, involve routine profiteering by rapacious businesses exploiting employees, consumers, and communities. As discussed in Chapter 4, the line between corporate self-interest and economic wilding is blurred in today's global economy, but not all profits arise out of exploitation and many profitable businesses are not engaged in economic wilding. Socially responsible or employee-owned businesses that add to social well-being by creating jobs, raising the standard of living of employees, improving the environment, and enhancing the quality of life of their customers may be highly profitable but are hardly wilders. Systemic connections exist between American capitalism and wilding, but not all forms of capitalism breed wilding.

Finally, not all crime, violence, or evil behavior is individualistic wilding. The horrific ethnic cleansing in Bosnia and the genocidal warfare in Rwanda constitute wilding by almost any definition, but such wilding is rooted in fierce and pathological tribal or communal loyalties and is hardly an expression of rampant individualism. Individualism and communitarianism can each generate their own forms of wilding; I focus on the individualistic variant in this book because it is the type endemic in the United States. This should not be viewed as a preference for the communitarian form, because wilding in many of the world's cruelest societies has its roots in the excesses of community. Wilding can be avoided only by respecting the rights of individuals and the needs for community, a balancing act too many societies have failed dismally to achieve.

The Two Americas: Are We All Wilders?

Although the wilding epidemic now infects almost every major American institution, cooperative behavior survives, and in every community one finds idealists, altruists, and a majority of citizens seeking to live lives guided by moral principles. Most Americans give money to charity and about half roll up their sleeves and volunteer or become social activists; these are among the many hopeful indications, discussed later in Chapter 9, that America can still purge itself of this epidemic.

For an analyst of wilding, there are two Americas: the America already seriously infected, which is the main subject of this book, and the America that has not yet succumbed and remains a civil society. The majority of ordinary Americans, it should be stressed, are part of the second America, and retain a moral compass and emotional sensibilities that inhibit severe wilding behavior. But as the epidemic continues to spread, individual interests increasingly override common purposes, and the self—rather than family or community—increasingly grabs center stage in both Americas. Not everyone will become a wilder, but nobody will be untouched by wilding culture.[20]

Wilders who catch the fever and play by the new rules profoundly infect their own vulnerable communities, families, and workplaces. One dangerous criminal on a block can make a community wild, inducing aggression, violence, and a fortress mentality among peaceable neighbors. A particularly competitive salesperson or account executive can transform an entire office into a jungle, because those who do not follow suit may be left sundered. The new ethos rewards the wilder and penalizes those who cling to civil behavior. One defense against wilding in modern America is to embrace it, spreading wilding behavior among people less disposed to be wilders and still struggling against wilding as a way of life.

Many Americans misread the epidemiology of AIDS as a problem of deviant and disadvantaged groups. They are at risk of making the same miscalculation about the wilding epidemic, to which no sector of the society has any immunity. Its ravages may be most eye-catching among the poor and downtrodden, but the virus afflicts the respected and the comfortable just as much; it exists in the genteel suburbs as well as the inner cities. Indeed, American wilding is, to a surprising degree, an affliction of the successful, in that the rich and powerful have written the wilding rules. It is ever more difficult to climb the ladder without internalizing those rules.

The progress of the wilding epidemic is shaped less by the percentage of sociopaths than by the sociopathy of society's elites and the rules of the success game they help to define. A wilding society is one where wilding is a route to the top, and where legitimate success becomes difficult to distinguish from the art of wilding within—or even outside of—the law.

The wilding epidemic is now seeping into America, mainly from the top. Although the majority of business and political leaders remain honest, a large and influential minority are not only serving as egregious role models but are rewriting the rules of the American success game in their own interest. CEOs who build their corporate fortunes on the backs of downsized workers at home and sweatshop workers abroad are re-creating the rules of last century's greed-soaked robber baron capitalism. Similarly, Presidents Reagan, Bush I, Clinton, and Bush II have all helped fuel the wilding crisis, partly by virtue of the corruption and scandals in their administrations, but more importantly through radical new policy directions.

Our current wilding crisis is rooted politically in the "free market" revolution that began with President Reagan. The Reagan revolution advanced the most ambitious class agenda of the rich in over a century, creating an innovative brew of market deregulation and individualistic ideology that helped fan the flames of wilding across the land. In the 1990s, a new Republican congressional majority led by Speaker Newt Gingrich, and the "new Democrats" led by President Clinton, launched their own wilding initiatives and raced against each other to dismantle the social programs that symbolize our commitment to the poor, the needy, and to each other. And at this writing, in 2003, President George W. Bush, despite his rhetoric of compassionate conservatism, promises to complete the revolution of greed that Reagan began.

Wilding and the New American Dream: Individualism Today and Yesterday

Many signs point to a corruption of the American Dream in our time.[21] Most Americans do not become killers to make it up the ladder or to hold on to what they have, but the traditional restraints on naked self-aggrandizement seem weaker—and the insatiability greater. Donald Trump, who by 1995 had made a major comeback and ruled vast gambling and real estate empires, is only one of the multimillionaire cultural heroes who define life as "The Art of the Deal" (the title of Trump's best-selling autobiography). Trump seems to feel no moral contradiction about building the most luxurious condominiums in history in a city teeming with homeless people. Trump writes triumphantly about the Trump Tower: "We positioned ourselves as the only place for a certain kind of very wealthy person to live—the hottest ticket in town. We were selling fantasy."[22]

The fantasy mushroomed in the late 1990s with young dot-com entrepreneurs dreaming of becoming millionaires before turning thirty. The "new economy" brought the age of "me.com" in which everyone looked for a fast fortune, whether by creating a new tech start-up or scoring big in day trading. Jonathan Lebed, a 15-year-old New Jersey surburban high school kid made over $800,000 day trading and recommending stocks on the Internet. In 2000, the Securities and Exchange Commission accused him of violating laws regulating stock promotions and made him return over $200,000. This didn't stop many of his fellow students and even many of his teachers from rushing to join him on a new Internet venture that might make them all rich.[23]

In 2001, David Callahan bemoaned the new ethos of greed: "The economy of the late 1990s offered the promise of such extraordinary wealth that it brought out the worst in people. . . . The ideal of working hard over many years to achieve wealth lost traction. The pressure to pursue wealth instead of other goals grew enormously as the media focussed on those winning big in the new economy. It became easy to feel that missing the gold rush was plain stupid." A young person himself, Callahan continues, "I've seen the resulting distortion of values everywhere in Generation X— my generation and in those coming after it. It's hard to stick to a goal related to something other than money. . . . Who wants to be a school teacher when you can be a millionaire."[24]

A new version of the American Dream has now emerged, more individualistic, expansive, and morally perverted than most of its predecessors. America has entered a new Gilded Age, where, as John Taylor writes, the celebration and "lure of wealth has overpowered conventional restraints."[25] Laurence Shames suggests that the name of the American game has become simply "more."[26]

Today's dot-commers and high rollers in Wall Street's famous investment banks are living out this new chapter of the American Dream. Youthful commodity traders fresh out of business school engage in feeding frenzies in the exchanges, pursuing quick fortunes "as if they'd invented the habit of more, when in fact they'd only inherited it the way a fetus picks up an addiction in the womb." The craving, Shames writes, is "there in the national bloodstream."[27] A dramatic model is Nicholas Leeson, the 27-year-old broker who in 1995 bankrupted the historic Baring's bank of London by losing his $27 billion gamble in the international derivatives market. Derivatives, a more recent variant of the 1980s junk-bond craze, are part of the global financial casino in which bankers bet on currency rates, stock prices, or pork bellies to win trillion-dollar jackpots. Many Wall Street players in the derivatives game turn to inside trading—and more serious crimes—when their risky ventures go bad. The notorious Billionaire Boys' Club—a group of youthful traders and investors—showed that respectable young men consumed by the Dream could become killers. And so, proved Mark Barton, could day traders who gamble big time. In 1999, Barton barged into the Atlanta offices of the day-trading firms where he had lost $450,000 and shot nine people in cold blood.

For less-privileged and especially for poor Americans, the new gilded Dream became a recipe for wilding based on collapsed possibilities. A dream of having more had been sustainable when the pie was growing, as it had been through most of American history. But when real income begins to decline for millions in the bottom half of America, an unprecedented development in the last decades of the twentieth century, an outsized Dream becomes illusion, inconsistent with the reality of most Americans' lives. Outsized Dream, downsized lives. To weave grandiose materialist dreams in an era of restricted opportunities is the ultimate recipe for social wilding.

A new age of limits and polarization in the early twenty-first century sets the stage for an advanced wilding crisis. In an America deeply divided by class, the American Dream, and especially the new gilded Dream, cannot be a common enterprise and is transformed into multiple wilding agendas, unleashing wilding among people at every station, but in different ways. Among those at the bottom, the Dream becomes pure illusion; wilding, whether dealing drugs or robbing banks, beckons as a fast track out of the ghetto and into the high life. Among the insecure and slipping great American middle class, wilding becomes a growth area for those who are endowed with classic American initiative and ingenuity and are unwilling to go down with their closing factories and downsized offices. For the professional and business classes at the top, wilding passes as professional ambition and proliferates as one or another variant of dedicated and untrammelled careerism. Ensconced inside heavily fortified suburban or gentrified enclaves, these elites also pioneer new forms of social wilding in what Robert Reich calls "a politics of secession," abandoning society itself as part of a panicky defense against the threat from the huge covetous majority left behind.[28] The wilding crisis, as we see below, arises partly out of a virulent new class politics.

The seeds of America's wilding plague were planted long before the current era. A century ago, Tocqueville observed that conditions in America led every "member of the community to be wrapped up in himself" and worried that "personal interest will become more than ever the principal, if not the sole spring" of American behavior.[29] Selfish and mean-spirited people can be found in every culture and every phase of history, and wilding, as I show in the next chapter, is certainly not a new phenomenon in American life. One of the world's most individualistic societies, America has long struggled to cope with high levels of violence, greed, political corruption, and other wilding outcroppings.

Over the last hundred years, American history can be read as a succession of wilding periods alternating with eras of civility. The robber baron era of the 1880s and 1890s, an age of spectacular economic and political wilding, was followed by the Progressive Era of the early twentieth century, in which moral forces reasserted themselves. The individualistic license of the 1920s, another era of economic and political wilding, this time epitomized by the Teapot Dome scandal, yielded to the New Deal era of the 1930s and 1940s, when America responded to the Great Depression with remarkable moral and community spirit. The moral idealism of a new generation of youth in the 1960s was followed by the explosion of political, economic, and social wilding in the current era.

American wilding is a timeless and enduring threat, linked to our national heritage and most basic values and institutions. Although we focus in this book on wilding today, the wilding problem riddles our history, for it is embedded in the origins of free-market capitalism and the individualistic culture that helped shape the American Dream and our own national character. What distinguishes the current epidemic is the subtle legitimation of wilding as it becomes part of the official religion in Washington; the severity of the wilding crisis in banking and commerce; the spread of wilding into universities, films, TV, popular music, and other vital cultural centers; and the subsequent penetration of wilding culture so deeply into the lives of the general population that society itself is now at risk.

Roots of Wilding: Durkheim, Marx, and the Sociological Eye

More than a century ago, the founders of sociology had their own intimations of a wilding crisis that could consume society. The great French thinker Émile Durkheim recognized that individualism was the rising culture of the modern age. While Durkheim believed that individualism could ultimately be a healing force, he also feared that it could poison the bonds that make social life possible. Karl Marx, who gave birth to a different school of sociology, believed that the economic individualism of capitalism might erode all forms of community and reduce human relations to a new lowest common denominator: the cash nexus.

Sociology arose as an inquiry into the dangers of modern individualism, which could potentially kill society itself. The prospect of the death of society gave birth to the question epitomized by the Ik: What makes society possible and prevents it from disintegrating into a mass of sociopathic and self-interested isolates? This core question of sociology has become the vital issue of our times.

Although sociology does not provide all the answers, it offers a compelling framework for understanding and potentially solving the wilding epidemic. Durkheim never heard of wilding or the Ik, but he focused like a laser on the coming crisis of community. Durkheim saw that the great transformation of the modern age was the breakdown of traditional social solidarity and the rise of an individual less enmeshed in community. In Durkheim's view egoism posed a grave danger, arising where "the individual is isolated because the bonds uniting him to other beings are slackened or broken" and the "bond which attaches him to society is itself slack." Such an individual, who finds no "meaning in genuinely collective activity," is primed for wilding, the pursuit of gain or pleasure at the expense of others with whom there is no sense of shared destiny.[30]

The other great danger is anomie, which Durkheim defined as a condition of societal normlessness that breeds crime and suicide. Anomie arises when social rules are absent or confusing and individuals are insufficiently integrated into families, neighborhoods, or churches to be regulated by their moral codes. Durkheim believed that modern individualistic societies were especially vulnerable to this kind of failure of socialization. As community declines, it leaves the individual without a moral compass, buffeted by disturbing and increasingly limitless "passions, without a curb to regulate them."[31] Anomie fuels instrumental wilding, making the individual more vulnerable to fantasies of limitless money and power. It also feeds expressive wilding of the O. J. Simpson variety, weakening the personal and community controls that sustain civilized values.[32]

Although Durkheim captured the kind of breakdown of community that is currently helping to breed the American wilding epidemic, he lacked the economic and political analysis that would help explain why wilding is startlingly pervasive among America's ruling elites and trickles down to the population at large. As I will argue in chapters to come, American wilding is a form of socially prescribed antisocial behavior, modeled by leaders and reinforced by the rules of our free-market game. As such, it reflects less the insufficient presence of society in individuals than overconformity to a society whose norms and values are socially dangerous.

Marx wrote that the market system "drowns the most heavenly ecstasies of religious fervor, of chivalrous enthusiasm, of philistine sentimentalism, in the icy water of egotistical calculation." In capitalism, from a Marxist perspective, wilding is less a failure of socialization than an expression of society's central norms. To turn a profit, even the most humane capitalist employer commodifies and exploits employees, playing by the market rules of competition and profit-maximization to buy and sell their labor power as cheaply as possible.[33]

The champions of Western capitalism—from Adam Smith to Milton Friedman—agree that self-interest is the engine of the system and individualism its official religion, but reject Marx's equation of a regime built around economic self-interest with exploitation and wilding. Marx was wrong, in fact, to assume that capitalism inevitably destroyed community and social values. In some national contexts, including Confucian Japan and social-democratic Sweden, the individualizing forces of the market are cushioned by cultures and governments that limit exploitation and help sustain community.

In the United States, however, rugged individualism has merged with free-market capitalism, creating a fertile brew for wilding. A Marxist view of institutionalized wilding—and of political and business elites as carriers of the virus—helps to correct the Durkheimian hint of wilding as deviance. Durkheim, in a major oversight, never recognized that egoism and anomie can themselves be seen as norms, culturally prescribed and accepted.[34]

This is a theoretical key to understanding wilding in America. Wilding partly reflects a weakened community less able to regulate its increasingly individualistic members. In this sense, the American wilder is the product of a declining society that is losing its authority to instill respect for social values and obligations.

But Marx's view of institutionalized wilding suggests that wilders can simultaneously be oversocialized, imbibing too deeply the core values of competition and profit-seeking in American capitalism. The idea of oversocialization, which I elaborate on in the next chapter, suggests not the failure of social authority but the wholesale indoctrination of societal values that can ultimately poison both the individual and society itself. As local communities weaken, giant corporations, including the media, advertising, and communications industries, shape the appetites, morality, and behavior of Americans ever more powerfully. For the rich and powerful, the dream of unlimited wealth and glamour, combined with the Reagan revolution of corporate deregulation and corporate welfare, opens up endless fantasies and opportunities. As Durkheim himself noted, when the ceiling on ordinary expectations is removed, the conventional restraints on pursuing them will also rapidly disappear. This produces socially prescribed anomie and wilding among elites that is based on unlimited possibilities.

A different version of socially prescribed wilding trickles down to everyone else. For those exposed to the same inflated dream of wealth, glamour, and power, but denied the means of achieving it, illegitimate means provide the only strategy to achieve socially approved goals. Whether involving petty or serious wilding, such behavior gradually permeates the population. Sociologist Robert Merton wrote that crime is a product of a disparity between goals and means. If that disparity becomes institutionalized, crime and other deviance are normalized, and antisocial behavior becomes common practice. Wilding itself becomes a societal way of life.

New economic realities, including the fact that the coming generation faces the prospect of living less well than its parents, could trigger a healthy national re-examination of our values, and the pursuit of a less materialistic and individualistic life. The polarization of wealth and opportunity could also prompt, before it is too late, a rethinking of our class divisions and economic system. But without such a rescripting of the American Dream and free-market system, the new circumstances create the specter of an American nightmare reminiscent of the Ik.

2

The Ultimate Wilders

Prisoners of the American Dream

Why should we be in such desperate haste to succeed? And in such desperate enterprises?

—Henry David Thoreau

On October 16, 2000, a North Carolina state jury formally indicted Deidre Lane for killing her husband, NFL running back Fred Lane. Prosecutors contend the motive was money. Deidre, who confessed to the murder but claimed it was in self-defense, stood to gain $5 million in life insurance from a policy on her husband's life issued in 1999.[1]

Two years earlier, in 1998, east Texas pharmacist Frederic Welborn Lunsford pleaded guilty to killing his wife of 14 years, Janice Pamela, by poisoning her with prescription medicine. One night, he gave her a large dose of methadone to induce a comalike sleep. He then shot her in the chest and slit her wrists to make it look as if she had committed suicide. Lunsford admitted the murder after his secret lover came forward and told police that he had talked about hiring someone to kill his wife. Lunsford told his mistress that he couldn't deal with the financial consequences of an impending divorce. He had paid child support for two children from a prior divorce and desperately feared being saddled with the costs of two more. It was easier to kill his wife than lose his kids and deal with the debt.[2]

A few years earlier, Pamela Smart, an ambitious, pretty New Hampshire high school media services director, seduced an adolescent student and persuaded him to help her kill Gregory Smart, her 24-year-old husband. After the murder, her teenage lover went to jail and Smart got thousands in insurance money. But she wasn't able to enjoy it for long because the real story finally leaked out from the boy and his friends. Smart was convicted of first-degree murder and sent to jail in Bedford Hills, New York, where she is incarcerated today. Still, Smart realized one of her ambitions—

to become famous. Hollywood made a movie, *To Die For*, about her venemous crime, with Nicole Kidman playing the "black widow," as women who kill their husbands for money are called.

All these killers are "ultimate wilders," Charles Stuart look-alikes prepared to do anything for money. Smart is most reminiscent of Stuart because she was ambitious, competitive, successful, and an "all-American" cheerleader and honors student. She aspired to be the next Barbara Walters, and many believed she'd make it. Smart, like Stuart, seemed the embodiment of the American Dream.

Sociologist C. Wright Mills argued that the sociological imagination connects personal biography to the social structure and culture of the times. In Chapter 1, I argued that our current wilding wave began around 1980, as a new American Dream and a new economy began to take form. Consider below three of the most infamous wilders who committed their crimes during this latest epidemic.

Robert Oakley Marshall: "Speed Demon on the Boulevard of Dreams"

After the prosecutor had summed up the case against their dad, and there could be no doubt in anyone's mind, not even their own, about the horrific fact that their father really had killed their mother, Roby and Chris, aged 20 and 19, were thinking the same thing. Their lives were a lie. They had always been envied, admired, privileged. They had had money and a perfect family. "How much in love with each other they'd all seemed. . . . The all-American family. The American Dream that came true."[3]

The sons now knew the truth—that their father, Rob, a spectacularly successful New Jersey life insurance salesman, had indeed arranged for professional assassins in Louisiana to come up on the night of September 7, 1984, to Atlantic City; that he had arranged the same night to drive his wife, Maria, to dinner at Harrah's in his Cadillac Eldorado. After dinner and wine and some late gambling in the casino, Rob had driven his sleepy wife back toward Toms River, had pulled off the parkway at the Oyster Creek picnic area to check out what he told Maria seemed to be a problem in the tire. Going out to examine the tire, he had waited for the paid executioners to steal up to the car, shoot Maria point-blank in the back, and swat Rob on the head to draw a little blood and make it look like a genuine robbery. (The Louisiana men had wanted to inflict a gunshot wound, but Rob had gone white and almost fainted—saying, "I'm not the one getting shot"—and insisted on only being hit on the head.) Rob had returned home looking strangely buoyant after his trauma, striking one detective as behaving more like a man ready to go out sailing on his yacht than someone who had just lost his wife. Rob Marshall had reason to feel a large burden had been lifted from his shoulders: He now stood to collect approximately $1.5 million from the insurance policy he had taken out on Maria, more than enough to clear $200,000 in gambling debts he owed in Atlantic City and to set himself up handsomely for his next steps on the ladder of the American Dream. He could pay off the mortgage, buy new cars for himself and each of his boys, and indulge in a whirlwind romance with his sexy mistress.

Rob Marshall had good cause to feel that the police would not come after him. Talking to Gene, his brother-in-law and a lawyer, who pointed out that it did not look especially good that he was deep in debt and stood to gain such a huge insurance payment, Rob responded that the police could not possibly suspect him. "I'm much too high up the civic ladder. My reputation in the community, in fact, places me beyond reproach."[4]

He was right about one thing: The police themselves called Rob a "pillar" of the community. Back in the early 1970s, Rob had quickly proved himself a sensational salesman, selling more than $2 million in life insurance in his first year; in his second he was again among the top 50 Provident Mutual Life salespeople in the country. Rob and his family had moved into a big house, and Rob drove around town in a flashy red Cadillac. Rob had also scored big in his private life, capturing Maria, a Philadelphia Main Line doctor's daughter who was exquisitely beautiful and always kept herself and her sons impeccably groomed. Maria was Rob's proudest possession. He loved her beauty. When he was arranging to have her killed, Rob told the executioners they must not mar Maria's looks; he could not stand that idea.[5]

Rob and Maria, Joe McGinniss writes, were like royalty in Toms River. One neighbor said they "seemed to have the ideal family and lifestyle. You know, like you'd see on TV."[6] Everyone admired how they looked; they also admired Rob's business success and the fact that the Marshalls "were always buying something new." They moved to a bigger house and joined the country club. Maria was invited to join Laurel Twigs, a prestigious charitable organization, and Rob became a mover and shaker in the Rotary Club, the United Way, and the country club.[7]

There was not much doubt about how Rob had gotten so far so fast. The man was *driven*, the most aggressive salesman Toms River had ever seen. Kevin Kelly, the prosecutor who had once bought insurance from

Rob, said Rob pushed through the deal while half his hamburger was still on his plate and the engine was still hot in the parking lot. "The guy could fit in three or four lunches a day, the way he hustled." His drive—and his ego—seemed as big as Donald Trump's, who happened to own the Atlantic City casinos where Rob gambled and where he staged Maria's last supper.[8]

Over the course of his nationally publicized trial, later celebrated in the TV miniseries *Blind Faith*, Rob's shameless behavior confirmed the nefarious picture of a sociopathic, greed-soaked personality painted by the prosecutor. In the first few weeks after the murder, Rob could barely conceal his excitement about his new freedom, not only making quick moves to get his hands on the money but also charming at least three different women into his wife's bed before he had figured out how to dispose of her remains. He staged a phony suicide attempt, giving himself the opportunity to leave "suicide tapes" by which he could publicly display his love of his kids and Maria. The fact is, as prosecutor Kevin Kelly showed, nobody close to Rob ever heard him weep or saw him show any real grief or sense of loss over Maria. In fact, Rob had indifferently left her ashes in a brown cardboard box in a drawer in the funeral home, while at the same time he put back on and prominently wore at the trial the gold wedding ring Maria had given him. Rob would embarrass his sons by his public demonstrations of his love for them, wearing signs for the cameras saying "I love you" even as he was desperately urging them to perjure themselves and risk jail to save his neck.

Prosecutor Kevin Kelly summed up Rob's personality: He's "self-centered, he's greedy, he's desperate, he's materialistic, and he's a liar. . . . [H]e will use anybody, he will say anything, and he will do anything—including use his own family—to get out from under." Rob was single-mindedly out for number one; he "loves no one but himself."[9] Kelly was not greatly exaggerating, but what he knew and did not say was that many of the same epithets could be applied to many other Toms River residents. The fact is, as one native observed, Rob was in many ways not a whole lot different from his neighbors. Rob's case, one resident wrote, was compelling precisely because there was an intimate connection between "the town's collective values and the story of Rob and Maria Marshall." Indeed, the spotlight on Rob—and the community's obsession with the trial—stemmed from the fact that it helped to bring into sharp definition what the community was really about.[10]

Toms River in the 1970s was full of people in a hurry, many of them like the Marshalls, recent immigrants to the town who were scurrying to cash in on one of the biggest booms on the New Jersey shore. Ocean County was the second-fastest-growing county in the country, which caused real estate values to soar and triggered spectacular business opportunities. The mostly blue-collar and lower-middle-class migrants who flocked to Toms River caught the fantastic entrepreneurial fever. Everyone in Toms River was suddenly making deals, and the limits on the money to be made evaporated. Since most people were new to the community, conspicuous consumption became the quickest way to become known and command respect. "I shop, therefore I am" became the Toms River credo long before it started showing up on bumper stickers around the country. Lots of Toms River folks were joining the country club and driving their Cadillacs up to Atlantic City at night, joining Rob for the big bets at the high-priced blackjack tables.

Rob was a hustler, but hustling was the name of the game in Toms River, just as it already was in Atlantic City and as it was increasingly becoming in Ronald Reagan's Washington and on Wall Street. Rob, a number of commentators observed, was remarkably tuned in to the spirit of his times. The commercials about getting yours and getting it now kept ringing in his ears. And as the 1980s progressed, Rob tuned in to bigger dreams than Toms River could offer. "See, all around Rob in the eighties," one old friend said, "everybody was scoring everything: sex, dope, big-money deals. At least, he thought so."[11] If those young kids out of business school could be making their first million on Wall Street before they were 30, Rob was missing something he deserved. As his success grew, so did his aspirations, his sense of deprivation, and his gambling debts. Like the country as a whole, Rob was going to leverage himself into a real fortune.

Yet if the resonance between Rob and the collective values of his time was electric, most people in Toms River and Atlantic City were not murdering their wives to cover their debts and advance one more step up the ladder. Rob was different, but mainly because he personified so purely and acted out so unrestrainedly the hungers driving his neighbors. Lots of others were dreaming the same big American Dream. But Rob was completely engulfed by it, his personality a machine perfectly dedicated to "making it." Rob was abnormal because the American Dream that was becoming the new standard had penetrated every fiber of his being, purging all traces of the emotional or moral sensibilities that restrained his neighbors. Rob's aggressiveness was startling even in an age of hustlers, his narcissism more extreme than that of most of his fellow travelers in the Me generation, and in an age of moral decline, his conscience was exceptionally elastic.

Undoubtedly, Rob's "abnormality" had roots in his past—perhaps in the Depression, which ruined his family and turned his father into an alcoholic; perhaps in his chronic sense of being an outsider, having moved at least 10 times before he was 16. But if Rob had not murdered his wife, he would never have come under the psychiatric microscope, because his extreme traits were exactly those that people on the way up were supposed to exhibit—and that would propel them to the top. For 15 years, Rob's "abnormality" had helped make him the biggest success in his community.

Rob got into trouble only because his dreams finally outstripped his own formidable capacities. He probably would not have killed Maria if he had not fallen so deeply into debt, and he might not have gotten into such debt if he had not been lured by the bigger dreams and looser moral sensibilities that his friends said had gotten under his skin and now possessed him. The reckless and grandiose entrepreneurial culture of Toms River that swept across America released the extremes in Rob's personality, nurturing his sense of himself as a legend in his own time, free to make his own rules and look after number one first. When he got into deep financial trouble, values and a culture that might have restrained him were not in place and his deep-seated potential for wilding was unleashed.

Them and Us: Violence and the Oversocialized American Character

Public reaction to ultimate wilders like Rob Marshall, Charles Stuart, and Pamela Smart has been schizophrenic. Utter shock that anyone could indifferently wipe out a wife, husband, mother, or child for money is linked with a sliver of recognition that there is something familiar about these killers. "The first thing people want to know," Alison Bass wrote in the *Boston Globe,* is "how could anyone so carefully and coolly plan the murder of a wife, a child, anyone?"[12] But the second, usually subliminal, question is, "Could my spouse do it?" or, even more subliminal, "Could I?"

Do ultimate wilders tell us something important about ourselves and our society, or are they just bizarre sideshows? Reassuring responses come from many commentators, such as psychiatrist Dr. Charles Ford, who believe that although people such as Rob Marshall, Charles Stuart, and Pamela Smart "on the surface look very normal," they are suffering from either mental illness or deep-seated "character disorders" such as narcissism or sociopathy, that radically differentiate "them" from "us."[13] Criminologists James Alan Fox and Jack Levin describe sociopaths such as Charles Stuart as people who "blend in well and function appropriately" but are "far from normal." Criminologists explain that sociopaths "know the right thing to do" to emulate the rest of us; they are consummate actors: "Sociopaths lie, manipulate, and deceive. They are good at it. Like actors, they play a role on the stage of life."[14]

When they murder, ultimate wilders clearly act differently from the majority of the population, but the clinical accounts of their character disorders do not provide a persuasive argument for the difference between "them" and "us" and make reassurances by psychological professionals ring hollow. The Bible of psychiatry, the *Diagnostic and Statistical Manual of the American Psychiatric Association,* defines narcissistic personality disorder as "[t]he tendency to exploit others to achieve one's own ends, to exaggerate achievements and talents, to feel entitled to and to crave constant attention and adulation."[15] Criminologists Fox and Levin define sociopaths as "self-centered, manipulative, possessive, envious, reckless, and unreliable. They demand special treatment and inordinate attention, often exaggerating their own importance. . . . On their way to the top, sociopaths ruthlessly step over their competitors without shame or guilt." These are common human frailties, and Fox and Levin acknowledge that they are widespread among Americans. In trying to predict when the difference between "them" and "us" emerges, Fox and Levin end up in another conundrum, for they acknowledge that most sociopaths rarely reach the point "at which they feel it necessary to kill. Most of them live ordinary lives." Distinguishing "them" from "us" then seems a bit like the dilemma American soldiers faced in Vietnam—trying to distinguish the guerrillas from the rest of the population.[16]

It is time for sociologists to apply the idea of sociopathy, a concept as useful for understanding a sick society as a sick psyche. A sociopathic society is one, like that of the Ik, marked by a collapse of moral order that results from the breakdown of community and the failure of institutions responsible for inspiring moral vision and creating and enforcing robust moral codes. In such a society, the national character-type tends toward sociopathy, and idealized behavior, although veiled in a rhetoric of morality, becomes blurred with antisocial egoism. The founders of modern sociology, especially Émile Durkheim, as noted in Chapter 1, worried that modernity threatened to turn the most developed industrial cultures into sociopathic cauldrons of raw egoism and anomie, and conceived of the sociological enterprise as an effort to understand how societies could find their moral compass and preserve themselves in the face of the sociopathic threat.

In sociopathic societies, the clinical effort to dissect the sociopathic personality cannot be separated from an analysis of national character and ideology. Rob Marshall, Charles Stuart, and Pamela Smart may be deranged, but their derangement mirrors a national disorder. As the United States enters the twenty-first century, the official religion of the free market increasingly sanctifies sociopathy in the guise of individual initiative, entrepreneurship, and "making it." As the American Dream becomes a recipe for wilding, clinicians and criminologists need to deepen their sociological understanding or they will continue to misread Marshall, Stuart, and Smart as a failure of socialization rather than a pathology of oversocialization. Marshall internalized too deeply the core American values of competitiveness and material success, discarding any other values that might interfere with personal ambitions. Marshall, Stuart, Smart, and other ultimate wilders are most interesting as prisoners of the same American Dream that compels the rest of us but does not consume us with quite the same intensity.

Lyle and Erik Menendez: A Family of Competitors

On the evening of August 20, 1989, as José Menendez was watching television in the spacious den of his $4-million Beverly Hills estate, he had reason to feel pretty good about his life. José was a perfectionist who, according to his older son, Lyle, felt he could never "do something well enough." But even José, with his high standards and consuming ambition, might have admitted that an impoverished immigrant who by age 45 had risen to become a millionaire in Hollywood's inner sanctum had not done too badly. He could count celebrities Barry Manilow, Kenny Rogers, and Sylvester Stallone as his friends. Founder and president of Live Entertainment, Inc., a successful national videocassette distributor, his was a Horatio Alger story come true. Journalist Pete Hamil wrote in *Esquire* magazine that José was a "glittering" testimony to the American Dream of the Reagan years.[17]

As he sat with his wife, Kitty, that evening, eating fresh berries and cream, José would certainly have gotten deep satisfaction from the comments of his fellow executive Ralph King, who eulogized José in the *Wall Street Journal* after his death as "by far the brightest, toughest businessman I have ever worked with," or of former Hertz chairman Robert Stone, who said he "had never known anyone who worked harder, worked toward more goals." José, according to Stone, probably "would have become president of the company" had he stayed at Hertz. Coming to the United States from Cuba at age 15, José had dedicated every ounce of his being to getting ahead, vowing to "develop strip malls" if that was what it took to "succeed by age thirty." He could not have been better psychologically equipped. He was an intensely aggressive and competitive man brimming with entrepreneurial energy. Straight out of accounting school, he had hustled from Coopers and Lybrand to a Chicago shipping firm to Hertz, and then to RCA, successfully signing performer José Feliciano. After being passed over for executive vice president at RCA, Menendez achieved a brilliant coup by creating Live Entertainment, Inc., the video arm of Carolco Pictures, on whose board he sat and which had gone big-time with its smash hit, *Rambo II*.[18]

Turning to his two handsome sons as they burst into the room, José could savor a different kind of pride. José had a burning desire to see his sons succeed as he had, and he had dedicated himself to that end with the same relentless passion with which he had pursued his business goals. He drilled Lyle and Erik for hours on the tennis courts and constantly exhorted them to outperform their peers on and off the court. "There is a lot of pressure," Erik said, "to be great." Lyle, aged 22, was to graduate soon from Princeton, and Erik, aged 19, who had gotten into UCLA, was talking about wanting to realize his father's own ambition of becoming the first Cuban-American U.S. senator.

José was probably more puzzled than frightened when he saw that Lyle and Erik were both carrying shotguns. But he had no time to ask questions. Within seconds of barging into the den, as police reconstruct the scene, the two sons had fired eight shots point-blank at their father and five at their mother. Just to make sure, they thrust the barrel of one gun into their father's mouth and blew off the back of his head. Police would later say that the scene was so gruesome that it could not possibly have been a Mafia hit, as some had first speculated, because Mob kills are "clean." Erik later told reporters that his parents' ravaged, blood-spattered, lifeless bodies "looked like wax."[19]

Lyle and Erik claimed that they had gone out that evening to see the James Bond film *License to Kill* but ended up seeing *Batman*. They came back late at night, they said, horrified to find the carnage at home. Neighbors reported that they heard the sons screaming and sobbing, presumably after discovering the bodies. But police suspected Lyle and Erik from the very beginning—and not only because, as District Attorney Ira Reiner put it, a $14-million estate provided "an ample motive." The boys were not able to produce ticket stubs for *Batman*, and police had found a shotgun shell casing in one of Lyle's jackets. Then investigators discovered that in high school two years earlier, Erik had co-written a play about a wealthy teenager who murders his parents for money, a creation that made his mother, who helped type the manuscript, proud of her son's gifts. But it was about six months later that police found the smoking gun they were seeking when they confiscated tapes of psychotherapy sessions with both boys that apparently offered direct evidence of their involvement in the crime.[20]

The Menendez brothers eventually confessed to the killings, acknowledging that they had followed through on a calculated plan to shoot their parents. But Lyle and Erik presented themselves in court not as brutal murderers but as innocent victims. They said they killed in self-defense, and because of years of emotional and sexual abuse. Erik claimed that his father had been sexually abusing him since he was 5 years old, forcing him repeatedly to have oral and anal sex.

The prosecution, however, as well as many followers of the trial, were skeptical about this "abuse excuse," noting accurately that it was one of the more fashionable and disturbing trends in legal defenses. It had cropped up in such infamous trials as the Bobbitt case, in which a sexually abused wife defended cutting off her husband's penis because he beat her. There were reasons to doubt the truth of the Menendez brothers' sexual abuse claims, among them the fact that in their time in psychotherapy the boys had never mentioned sexual abuse to their therapist, Dr. L. Jerome Oziel, who was the one to initially get (and tape) the boys' murder confession. Erik and Lyle had given Dr. Oziel written permission when they entered therapy to share their confidences with their parents, an unlikely act for young men who would presumably be using the therapy to discuss their parents' alleged mental, physical, and sexual abuse. In addition, the abuse defense was introduced late in the game, many months after the killings and shortly before the trial opened. Family members and others who had known the family well and were familiar with José's many mistresses and affairs, were reported to be incredulous, partly because none of them had ever heard any whisper of this other side of the macho José's sexual life.

Even if José had sexually abused his sons, such abuse would neither justify the killings nor constitute proof of the real motive of the shootings. There were other ways for these smart and wealthy young men to defend themselves and escape the family's oppressive yoke, including running away and assuming new identities, seeking shelter with friends, relatives, or protective social service agencies, or going off to boarding school and college, as Lyle, in fact, had done. But all of these strategies would probably have cost Lyle and Erik their inheritance and certainly would not have given them immediate access to their parents' huge estate.

The remarkable behavior of Lyle and Erik after the killings offers the most revealing clues about why they committed them. Neither boy wasted any time. Lyle dropped out of Princeton and, after flirting with the idea of a professional tennis career (he had once ranked 36th in the U.S. juniors), decided "to build a business empire from the ground up." Taking his share of an initial $400,000 insurance payment, he bought Chuck's Spring Street Café, a popular student hangout near the Princeton campus specializing in fried chicken. Lyle immediately began drafting plans to open franchises in other states as part of a nationwide chain. His entrepreneurial ambitions extended far beyond restaurants. Lyle began traveling widely to help realize his dream of making a "fortune in, among other things, show business and real estate." He founded Investment Enterprises, a financing shell for channeling the millions of dollars he would inherit into quick, high-yield returns.[21]

Erik, however, was serious about professional tennis, immediately dropping out of UCLA and hiring a professional tennis coach for $50,000 a year. He moved into the exclusive Marina City Club Towers, a glamorous ocean-side setting south of Los Angeles. Erik worked as hard at his tennis career as Lyle did at his restaurant and real estate ventures, practicing for hours on the court and taking his coach along to boost his performance in tournaments. Erik, however, did not limit himself to a future in tennis. Still proud of his earlier murder script, he believed he had a spectacular future as a screenwriter. In his spare time, he worked on his plays and poetry. He told his roommate at Marina that he was confident he would "produce an unbelievable script."[22]

It took little imagination to view the killings, as the police did, as a grand entrepreneurial scheme, an ironic testimony to the grip of a father's deepest values on the minds of his sons. More than anything else, José had wanted Erik and Lyle to follow in his footsteps and live out the American Dream that had guided his own life. He had raised them to be aggressive competitors like himself who would seize every opportunity to get ahead and make something of themselves. "He wanted us," Erik said, "to be exactly like him." Lyle and Erik converted patricide into a carefully planned strategy for catapulting their careers into fast-forward. In a bizarre twist, they proved how fully they had imbibed their father's values and opened themselves to the entrepreneurial spirit of the decade that shaped them.[23]

Lyle and Erik were themselves fully aware of the power of their ties to the father they had killed. "We are prototypes of my father," Erik pronounced after the shootings. He added, "I'm not going to live my life for my father, but I think his dreams are what I want to achieve. I feel he's in me, pushing me." As for Lyle, he all but admitted that his whole life had been a preparation for the day when he could jump into his father's shoes. Two days after the killings, Lyle told his friend Glen Stevens, who commented on how well Lyle seemed to be holding up, "I've been waiting so long to be in this position." Later, commenting on his ambitious business plans, Lyle said, "I just entered into my father's mode."[24]

The Menendez brothers had become prisoners of the American Dream, captives of their father's extravagant ambitions. Theirs may have been "ambition gone berserk," as a *Wall Street Journal* report put it, but it represented less a crazy break from reality than an excessive vulnerability to the culture around them.[25] The messages coming from their father, from Beverly Hills, from Princeton, and from Wall Street were telling them the same thing: Money is good, more money is better, and they had only themselves to blame if they did not seize every opportunity to strike it rich. The seductive power of these messages on the boys is apparent in their uncontrolled orgy of spending after getting the first cut of their inheritance. Lyle bought a new Porsche, which was not especially unusual, but his spending on clothes was extravagant, even for Princeton. Upscale clothier Stuart Lindner remembers Lyle coming into his store "dressed in an expensive black cashmere jacket and wearing a Rolex watch," which Lindner priced at about $15,000. On that occasion, Lyle bought some $600 worth of clothes, including five $90 silk shirts. "We've had bigger sales," Lindner said, "but not in four minutes."[26]

The sons worshiped the same god as their father, but they gave the family religion a new spin. They had grown up in the era of Donald Trump and Bill Gates, who made their father's career path seem slow and his fortune paltry. Lyle told Venanzia Momo, owner of a Princeton pizza parlor Lyle tried to buy, that he did not want to have to struggle like his father had to succeed. "He said he wanted to do it faster and quicker," Momo said. "He said he had a better way."[27]

The seeds of Lyle's and Erik's ultimate wilding could be seen in a trail of small wildings reflecting the casual morality of the quick-money culture that engulfed them. Even as an adolescent, Lyle frequently went on spending binges, once running up a huge hotel bill in Tucson that his father had to cover. He racked up so many traffic violations that his license was suspended twice, and several times he got into trouble with the police during his travels in Italy. At Princeton, he copied a fellow psychology student's lab report and was told he could leave voluntarily or be expelled. Meanwhile, Erik also had brushes with the law, ending up in juvenile court on a number of occasions. José, however, was always there to bail the boys out, perhaps a fatal source of support, for it may well have been that their success in getting out of small jams helped persuade them that they could also get away with killing.

The Menendez case "speaks to every parent," says television producer Steven White. "Matricide and patricide go back to Greek drama." But Lyle and Erik are products of America. Their abnormality lies most of all in their uncritical receptivity to the "look after number one" message at the heart of contemporary American life. Lyle's and Erik's pathology was that they allowed themselves to be socialized so completely. They lacked the capacity to resist their father's dreams and the current era's mesmerizing obsession with money. What José had not realized was that it was not his children's ambition he had to cultivate—the larger culture would see to that—but the tender sentiments and moral sensibilities that might have prevented their ambition from metastasizing into a cancer of wilding.

Then and Now: An American Tragedy

In 1925, *An American Tragedy*, by Theodore Dreiser, was published. One of the country's great works of literature, it is about a young man, Clyde Griffiths, who plots to kill his pregnant girlfriend, Roberta, so that he can take up with a woman who is rich and well connected. The story is based on a real murder committed in 1906 by Chester Gillette, a New Yorker who drowned his pregnant girlfriend to be free to pursue a woman in high society. The striking resemblance of Dreiser's protagonist to both Lyle and Erik Menendez, and to other contemporary men in a hurry such as Charles Stuart and Rob Marshall, suggests that wilding, even ultimate wilding, is not new. But if the parallels tell us something important about the deep historical roots of American wilding, there are also noteworthy contrasts that hint at how the virus has mutated for the worse.

Like Erik and Lyle, Clyde was an authentic prisoner of the American Dream (as, presumably, was the real Chester Gillette, for, as H. L. Mencken notes, Dreiser stayed "close to the facts and came close to a literal reporting"). When Dreiser described Clyde as "bewitched" by wealth, as a personification of desire for all the glitter and beauty that money can buy, he could have been describing Erik and Lyle. Indeed, Dreiser saw young Clyde as so vulnerable to the seductive temptations that surrounded him, so helpless in the face of the material pleasures just beyond his reach, that Dreiser asked whether the real guilt for the crime lay not with Clyde but with the culture that debased him. Perhaps future novelists or historians will instructively engage the same question about the Menendez brothers, whose vulnerability to modern capitalist seduction is one of the most poignant aspects of their identity.

Dreiser selected the Gillette case, as critic Lawrence Hussman informs us, because he considered it "typical enough to warrant treatment as particularly American." Dreiser recognized that whatever psychological pathology was involved could be understood only in the context of a diagnosis of the health of American society and an inquiry into the moral ambiguity of the American Dream. *An American Tragedy* was compelling to millions of Americans in the 1920s because it held up a mirror in which they could see their collective reflection. The novel's success suggests that there was something of Clyde in many Americans of his era, which tells us how deeply the wilding virus had already insinuated itself into American life. Indeed, as early as the robber baron era of the late 1800s, the wilding streak in American culture had become too obvious to ignore, a matter of preoccupation for satirist Mark Twain, philosopher Henry David Thoreau, and critic Lincoln Steffens.[28]

Yet if Dreiser's work suggests that wilding defines a continuity, not a break, in American life, it also hints at how things have changed. Unlike Rob Marshall or Erik and Lyle Menendez, Clyde could not actually go through with his diabolical scheme. After becoming obsessed with plans to kill his girlfriend, he lures her into a canoe with the intent of drowning her, but, whether out of weakness or moral compunction, he cannot do it. His problem is solved only because she accidentally falls into the water, along with Clyde himself. Clyde does not try to save her, partly because he is afraid that her thrashing about will drown him, too, but that is quite different from deliberate murder. Perhaps in the America of 1925 it was still not credible to Dreiser or his audience that anyone could actually carry out such a crime, although the real Chester Gillette was only one of a number of such accused killers in the first quarter of the twentieth century. While such murders still shock the public, Americans today, according to pollsters, not only believe that such crimes can be committed but, as noted earlier, worry whether their spouses, or they themselves, could succumb to the impulse.

That the constraints on wilding may have weakened over the last 75 years is suggested further by the centrality of the theme of guilt and moral responsibility in Dreiser's work. Clyde is a morally weak character, but he is not entirely devoid of conscience. After Roberta's death, Clyde is not able to absolve himself of responsibility because he is plagued by the question of whether he was guilty of not trying to save her. In contrast, the most extraordinary aspect of Rob Marshall and the Menendez brothers is their apparent lack of remorse. Friends of Rob Marshall, Erik and Lyle Menendez, Pamela Smart, and Charles Stuart commented on how well they looked after the killings; it was widely reported that they all seemed happier and better adjusted after their violent deeds and never appeared to suffer even twinges of conscience.

Dreiser's *An America Tragedy* is ultimately an indictment of the American Dream. The "primary message of the book," Lawrence Hussman reminds us, concerns the "destructive materialistic goals" that obsess Clyde and drive him to his murderous plot. Dreiser refused to accept that the evil could be explained away by Clyde's moral weakness or some presumed individual psychopathology; it was only the inability to question "some of the basic assumptions on which American society is based" that could lead anyone to that line of thinking. Dreiser himself concluded that Clyde had to be held morally accountable but that society was the ultimate perpetrator of the crime. He implicitly instructed his readers that such American tragedies would recur until the country finally triumphed over its obsessions with materialism and ego and rediscovered its moral compass.

Dreiser's musings on the American Dream remain stunningly relevant today, and the book is an eerie prophecy of current cases of wilding. But if Dreiser saw how the American Dream of his era could beget extreme individual wilding, he could not have foreseen the historical developments that have made the dream a recipe for a wilding epidemic. In Dreiser's day, the "American Century" was dawning on a glorious future; the prosperity of the 1920s was a harbinger of a new era of plenty in which all Americans could reasonably look forward to their share of an apparently endlessly expanding pie. Despite the dark side of the materialistic preoccupation, which divided people as they competed for the biggest slices, the Dream also brought Americans together, for as long as the pie was growing, everybody could win.

It took a new age of limits and decline, during which growing numbers of Americans would see their share of the pie shrinking and others see it permanently removed from the table, to set the stage for a full-blown wilding epidemic. Dreiser saw a foreshadowing of this in the Great Depression, which turned him toward socialism. But America pulled together in the 1930s, and the wilding virus was kept largely in check, as I discuss in Chapter 9. It would take a very different set of economic and political reversals, half a century later, to fuel the kind of wilding epidemic that Dreiser vaguely anticipated but never experienced.

It is apt testimony to Dreiser, as well as to the ferocious spread of the epidemic he could only dimly envisage, to mention in conclusion the rapidly growing crowd of modern-day Chester Gillettes. In addition to the Menendez brothers, Charles Stuart is among the most remarkable Gillette "look-alikes," not only because he killed his pregnant wife but because, like Chester, he was from a working-class background and disposed of his wife because she had become an impediment to his upward mobility. Stuart, of course, trumped Gillette's achievement by collecting several hundred thousand dollars in insurance money.

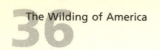

Susan Smith: Infanticide and the Honor Student

Susan Smith, now serving a life sentence in prison, hauntingly evokes Dreiser's character and theme. Smith is the young mother from Union, South Carolina, who confessed to strapping her two young sons—Michael, aged 3, and Alex, aged 14 months—into their car seats in her Mazda and driving the car onto a boat ramp leading into John D. Long Lake. She watched as the vehicle rolled into the water, carrying her two trusting infants to a grave at the bottom of the lake. The car sank slowly, still floating as the infants cried plaintively for their mother, who had run off to give her alibi to police.

Because Smith initially told police that the children had been kidnapped by a gun-toting black man, reporters compared her to Charles Stuart, who had concocted a similar racist story to throw off Boston police. Like Stuart, Smith triggered a national firestorm of self-examination. Americans everywhere wondered how a hardworking, church-going, honor society graduate in South Carolina's "City of Hospitality" could commit such a horrifying double murder.

Pundits and politicians offered their own explanations, including former Speaker of the U.S. House of Representatives Newt Gingrich, who at the time of the killings on October 25, 1994, was one of the most powerful politicians in America. Gingrich said the Smith murders showed "the sickness of our society" and was a "reason to vote Republican." But Gingrich, once a history professor, should have noticed the resemblance of Smith to Chester Gillette and realized that both Smith and Gillette had deeply imbibed the intensely individualistic version of the American Dream that Gingrich was selling.[29]

The relevance of Dreiser's novel and the American Dream to the Smith saga began with Smith's mother, Linda Sue, who in 1977 divorced her first husband, a blue-collar worker named Harry Ray Vaughan, to marry a stockbroker. Vaughan, Susan Smith's father, committed suicide a year after Linda Sue left him to "marry up."

Susan Smith's romantic ambitions resemble her mother's and are intimately tied to the murders. Shortly before the killings, Smith had separated from her own blue-collar husband and had started to date Tom Findlay, the wealthy son of a corporate raider. Tom's father owned the textile factory where Susan worked as a secretary. Smith was struggling financially, living on $125 a week of child support and a $325 weekly salary; she found it hard to meet her $344 monthly payments on her red-brick house. Susan dreamed of marrying Tom, who lived in a plush mansion called "the Castle." Tom, who was known to secretaries in the office as "the Catch," was feverishly pursued by many local women, and he complained to one friend not long before the killing, "Why can't I meet a nice single woman? Everyone at work wants to go out with me because of my money. But I don't want a woman with children—there are so many complications."[30]

Police regard the triggering event as the letter Tom sent Susan on October 18, in which he broke off their relationship, explaining that he "did not want the responsibility of children." Susan got painful evidence of Tom's seriousness about leaving and enjoying a less encumbered life when, only hours before she killed the children who had become the obstruction to her dreams, she found Tom in a bar flirting with three pretty single women.

After her confession, speculation in Union was rife that she did it for the money. In her confession, she wrote that she had "never been so low" because of her financial problems and that Findlay's rejection meant the loss not only of love but of the wealthiest man in the county. Police believed that Smith's desperation "to jump from the listing boat of the working class" appeared to be "a major motive" for her crime.[31]

There are haunting similarities with the Dreiser story, down to the detail of drowning as the way to free oneself for marrying up. Like Gillette, Susan and her mother both saw marriage as their path to the American Dream. Known in high school as the most "all-American," Susan found it too painful to see her dream slip away. Wealthy Tom Findlay was the ticket, and Susan saw no way to keep him other than killing her own children.

Susan Smith and the whole rogues' gallery of modern-day Dreiser characters are just the tip of the iceberg, not only of the larger wilding epidemic but of the roster of ultimate wilders, male and female, rich and poor, who are now grabbing headlines. Experts conservatively estimate that hundreds of such calculated, cold-blooded family murders for money have taken place in the past decade. What is striking is not just the numbers, but the percentage of those who were described by friends, associates, and the police as all-American types, defying the suspicion of many because they so purely embodied the qualities and the success that Americans idealize. Most Americans, of course, do not become killers, but as we see in the next chapter, an epidemic of lesser wilding has consumed much of popular culture and marks the lives of millions of ordinary Americans.

3

Cheaters, Cynics, Dot-Commers, and Survivors

Wilding Culture in the Media and Everyday Life

This whole world is wild at heart and weird on top.
—"Lula" in *Wild at Heart,* 1990

In September 2000, five teenagers in Queens, New York, were arrested for ordering take-out food from a Chinese restaurant and allegedly bludgeoning the owner to death when he personally delivered the order. They had no grudge against the owner; they just killed, police said, for a free meal of shrimp egg foo yung and chicken with broccoli. A few months later in Reading, Massachusetts, near Boston, one hockey dad assaulted and killed another dad, the latest in a string of attacks across the country by fathers against coaches, players, and other parents. On December 4, 2000, Shirley Henson, 41, from a suburb of Birmingham, Alabama, was sentenced to a 13-year jail sentence after shooting to death another driver, Gina Foster, a 34-year-old mother of three, in an infamous incident of road rage.[1] On June 24, 2003, Anna Gitlin, 25, who was angry about being held up in traffic after a fatal accident in Weymouth, Massachusetts, yelled at a police officer, "I don't care who [expletive] died. I'm more important." She was later charged with attempted murder of the officer when her car struck him, putting him in the hospital.[2]

But it is perhaps not such extreme acts of wilding but the small wildings that ripple through our daily experiences that are most revealing. *Boston Globe* columnist Susan Trausch satirizes her own propensity for wilding: "An extra 10 bucks dropped out of the automatic teller machine the other day and I didn't give it back." There were, after all, Trausch explains, "no guards. No middleman. . . . The machine doesn't ask questions." Trausch "grabbed the bills" and stifled "the impulse to shout, 'I won!'" Later, she asks herself, "Is this why the world is a mess? People don't want to be chumps so they say, 'I'll get mine now,' and then they grab an illicit brownie from the pastry tray of life. And oh, the noise we make if we don't get what we consider ours! If, for instance, only forty dollars had come out of the slot instead of fifty dollars, my outrage would have echoed in the aisles from aerosols to zucchini." But beating the system "made me want to play again," Trausch admits. "Maybe there was a gear loose. Maybe hundreds of dollars would come out." Trausch concludes that although she'd "like to report that at least the illicit money went to charity, it didn't. I blew it on lottery tickets."[3]

Trausch's lingering moral pangs are quite unusual. One sociologist laughed after reading her story, speculating that he and most other Americans would have pocketed the illicit greenbacks without a second thought, with no flickering of the conscience whatsoever. According to Queens, New York, school board member Jimmy Sullivan, a streetwise, savvy observer of American life, "Everybody cheats." It "isn't just some people," Sullivan emphasizes pointedly, "It's 95 percent of the people. Some cheat a little. Some cheat a lot. You work in an office, you take home supplies. People work at a construction site, they take home two-by-fours. Unfortunately, we've become a nation of petty crooks." Admitting to a reporter that his main concern as a school board official was patronage jobs for his "people"—white political cronies in his clubhouse—Sullivan makes no apologies. Everybody is doing it, cheating to get theirs, especially now that times are getting tougher. Sullivan certainly knows what he's talking about, at least regarding the New York City school system, where three-quarters of the city's school boards have been under investigation and half are believed to be corrupt. Sullivan himself was manipulating a multimillion-dollar budget to build his own corrupt school fiefdom. Sullivan explains, "We're a nation of fucks and gangsters because that's what we glorify in Americana." It's all part of the American Dream today.[4]

Sullivan pleaded guilty to using coercion to support institutionalized cronyism. He had not counted on the fact that there are still honest people like his school superintendent, Coleman Genn, who switched from working with Sullivan to wearing a hidden microphone for an independent commission investigating school corruption. Genn is part of the "second America" discussed in Chapter 1, the majority of Americans who have been touched but not debased by the wilding epidemic and continue to struggle honorably to maintain their integrity. Sullivan, nonetheless, put his finger on a contradiction that was tearing America apart. The pushers of dreams, the creators of "Americana," are feverishly selling the high-roller version of the American Dream in movies, magazines, and videos. While Americans are being willingly seduced, swimming in exquisitely alluring images of the pleasures only money can buy, money itself is get-

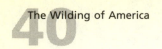
ting harder to come by for a large percentage of the population. As Americans dream big, economic shadows are lengthening and darkening. This contradiction between the glamorous life on the screen and the contrasting opportunities of real life has the potential to spread the epidemic deeply into the "second America" that, until now, has kept it at bay.

Temptation and Survival: Reality TV and the Ik-ing of America

If the ratings are to be believed, millions of us are addicted to reality TV. *Survivor* was the biggest hit of recent years, and copycat shows like *The Mole* and *Temptation Island* were also very popular. *Survivor II: The Australian Outback,* drew 30 million viewers in its first episode in 2001.

Richard Hatch, the now rich and famous winner of the original *Survivor,* symbolizes what reality TV is all about. Hatch never concealed his intention to win the million-dollar prize by remaining completely emotionally detached from everyone else. While others might find it difficult to repress real feelings for other players, Hatch was the consummate strategist and schemer. Drawing on his skills as a management consultant, he seemed to effortlessly build alliances with other participants while plotting how to dispense with each of them.

The subtext of *Survivor* is that if you want to survive and make large amounts of money, you have to learn how to manipulate people even as you partner with them. The manipulation is ruthless, since it requires throwing people off the island—a kind of mirroring on TV of the culture of downsizing that prevails in U.S. business. Robert Allen, the CEO of AT&T who laid off 70,000 workers while raising his own salary by millions, said that he "felt good about himself" because he was just looking after business—and succeeding.[5] All *Survivor* participants have to buy into a similar premise: that it is necessary to cultivate strategies for eliminating others on the team while plotting a path of success. Inflicting harm on your own teammates becomes not only essential but virtuous. Perhaps only a business culture based on big money and disposable labor could create a TV concept quite like *Survivor.*

The original *Survivor* series seemed almost benign, however, compared to *Survivor II.* Hatch "would have gotten eaten alive" by the *Survivor II* players, according to one of the show's hosts. This was intended to be a meaner *Survivor*, with what the show's creator, Mark Burnett, calls "real suffering." "The level of suffering in this season—it would make you cry," Burnett said. He was talking about physical suffering, but the show's commentary also suggests suffering of the soul.[6]

Other reality TV programs play off the basic formula of *Survivor* but are even meaner. *The Mole* was based on a surreptitious wilder who doesn't reveal his identity while sabotaging others. Hatch may have acted like a mole, but he was upfront about his intentions.

In *Temptation Island,* another hit show, the whole point was to test and subvert real-life relationships by enticing participants into infidelity with sexy other partners, with millions of viewers as titillated voyeurs. Tammy, a 27-year-old banker who is an addicted fan, says, "It seems so wrong to me, this whole concept of bringing these singles in to tempt the couples. But it's kind of like a car accident. I couldn't stop watching." Getting rid of people is in the mix here, too, since *Temptation Island* not only plays off the disposability of modern relationships (mates as live-in temps) but also involves repeated votes by participants to jettison others off the show.[7]

Temptation Island is also a twisted mirror image of *Who Wants to Marry a Millionaire?* Millionaire Rick Rockwell offered millions to a contestant who would actually marry him on TV. While *Temptation Island* broke relationships up through seduction and intrigue, *Millionaire* presented relationships as a strategy for getting rich. Darva Conger, the beautiful blonde nurse who married Rockwell on air, broke down and left him almost immediately, proving that the whole concept was somehow inhuman. But she kept the car she won, went on to pose nude, and turned herself into a celebrity.

The parallels between reality TV and the Ik are almost too obvious to mention. Among the Ik, survival is the only game in town. Relationships are pure manipulation and love is seen as absurd, an impediment to staying alive. The Ik have learned to get their greatest pleasure from duping and betraying their neighbors; every Ik is a cynical strategist, and Richard Hatch would find himself strangely at home among them.

Reality TV, in fact, creates a virtual culture that clones the wilding culture of the Ik. The only way to survive on *Survivor* is to act like an Ik, that is, to find a way to cheat and ultimately dispose of everyone around you. Among the Ik, this is necessary because everyone is a competitor for the food one needs to stay alive—and therefore it's kill or be killed. On *Survivor*, the survival strategy is essentially the same because the producers wrote the rules that way. The question is why the scenario works in the richest countries in history, a matter to be addressed shortly. Suffice it to say here that *Survivor* sells because it mirrors the survival strategy that millions of Americans have embraced.

Downtime: A New Wilding Recipe

As the price of happiness ratchets up, the ability of the average American to pay is falling. The great contradiction of today—and a recipe exquisitely designed for wilding—may be the increasing gap between bigger American appetites and shrinking American wallets.

The 1990s were billed as one of the great economic booms in history. The new dot-com economy, with its combination of magical technology and ruthless global corporate restructuring, helped to fuel the creation of astonishing new wealth. Many college students, like other young Americans, came to believe that they should be rich by 30, that this was their birthright, and that they had a golden future as millionaire dot-com entrepreneurs.

But the collapse of the dot-com economy and the high-tech Nasdaq in 2000, and the serious economic slowdown that followed, put the fabled new economy in a different light. The fantasy that everyone can become rich in the information economy soured in the new reality, and many wonder whether they will keep their jobs or be able to meet their rent and pay off their credit cards. We also learned that the boom never really did reach millions of Americans, since the bulk of the new wealth created in the 1990s was pocketed mainly by the very rich. Moreover, much of the new wealth turned out to be pure illusion, paper wealth that could vanish as magically as it had appeared.

A look back into recent economic history shows that the boom was always contradictory, putting the bigger dreams of most Americans on a collision course with the reality of the American economy. In 1973, for the first time ever, the real wages of the American worker began falling. By 1998, the real wages of the average American worker and the real income of the typical U.S. household had barely risen at all. In other words, 25 years of the Reagan and Clinton "booms" had done very little in real economic terms to help the ordinary American, a sad reality compounded by a big increase in job insecurity and a decrease in pension plans, health coverage, and other employee benefits.[8]

As Americans were learning to dream big, only a tiny fraction actually could afford to live big. The richest 1 percent of Americans creamed off most of the new wealth created by the new economy. The escalation of Bill Gates's net wealth to $100 billion in 2000—more than the combined wealth of nearly 100 million less fortunate Americans—hints at what was happening. Although wealth was being created rapidly, it was being distributed more unequally than at any time since the 1920s. By 1996, the

United States had become the most economically unequal country in the developed world, and the richest 1 percent owned more than 40 percent of the nation's wealth, a near record high. By 2000, U.S. median wages had declined well beyond those of most European countries, and the U.S. rate of poverty was triple that in northern Europe. Much of this decline reflected the successful attack on unions unleashed by President Reagan in 1981 and taken up enthusiastically by George W. Bush. Corporations have exploited labor weakness in the new global economy by rushing to find cheap labor overseas while breaking union contracts and cutting wages and benefits at home.[9]

While much of the boom has always been an illusion for ordinary Americans, they continue to be glued to the Dream Machine, creating the paradox that *Business Week* calls the "money illusion." They keep spending as if they are "getting the kind of real raises" that they used to get "in the 1960s." Something is profoundly out of kilter, the magazine suggests, because in a period of "crushing new constraints, the average American appears unable to lower his sights."[10]

Of course, the contradiction cuts more or less deeply depending on where the dreamer sits on the economic ladder. For those on top, whether business executives or fabled dot-commers, there is the problem, as the *New York Times* reported, of "feeling poor on $600,000 a year." The *Times* describes the misery of young Wall Street financiers and New York doctors and lawyers who feel strapped by the costs of their million-dollar co-ops. The pain is tolerable, however, as author Kevin Phillips writes, because Reaganomics (and Clintonomics) unleashed an upsurge of riches to the wealthy that "has not been seen since the late nineteenth century, the era of the Vanderbilts, Morgans, and Rockefellers." As the economy declines, the rich can keep dreaming big dreams.[11]

Where the contradiction draws blood is at the bottom. The poor, no less than the rich, stay tuned in to the Dream Machine in bad times as well as good. They are always the "last hired and the first fired," so every business cycle wreaks havoc with their dreams. Their boats did not rise with the Clinton boom and they got dangerously poorer, partly due to the cutting of the safety net under Reagan and the first Bush, partly due to Clinton's willingness to follow the leadership of Speaker Newt Gingrich and his Republican colleagues in shredding it further. After Clinton's dismantling of welfare, millions of the poor were left without housing, medical care, jobs, or educational opportunity; six million children—one of every four kids under 6 years of age in America—were officially poor. Mired in third world conditions of poverty while video-bombarded with first world dreams, rarely has a population suffered a greater gap between socially cultivated appetites and socially available opportunities.

Blood has been drawn in the great American middle as well. As they work longer and harder to get their share of the Dream, middle-class Americans are sinking. *Business Week* says that Joe Sixpack "plunged into debt, thinking 'Buy now, before the price goes up again.' With a little luck, he figured, his next raise would keep the credit-card bills and the mortgage covered."[12]

Unable to "lower his sights," Joe kept "borrowing. He now own[ed] a house, a big Japanese color TV and VCR, an American car, and a Korean personal computer—all bought on credit." By now, Joe had 10 credit cards, which he used to live well above his means, spending $1.03 or more for every $1.00 he earned. This credit-financed binge gave Joe the illusion of living the American Dream, and he wasn't alone: All across America consumers were piling up unprecedented credit-card debt, with the number of Americans declaring bankruptcy in 2000 about double that in 1990. The transfer of debt from government to ordinary citizens has been one of the great revolutions in the new economy.

Joe Sixpack's wife is working, which helps pay for the "children's orthodontist bills and family entertainment, but it falls short of what they'll need to send the kids to college." Judith Bateman, the wife of a Michigan Bell Telephone dispatcher, told *Business Week* that she and her husband run a big weekly "deficit, but until times get better, which she keeps hoping will happen, she says, 'We enter a lot of sweepstakes.' "[13]

Young and Wild: Drinking, Cheating, and Other Campus Sports

The young are among the more exuberant wilders in America. Progeny of the Reagan–Bush I–Clinton–Bush II era and the most vulnerable to the slings and arrows of economic fortune, they are an ominous harbinger of America's future.

Boston University professors Donald Kanter and Philip Mirvis report that a clear majority of youth under age 24, in contrast to only 43 percent of the population as a whole, are "unvarnished cynics" who view "selfishness as fundamental to people's character." Most students do not disagree with this assessment of their generation. On the first day of one semester, I asked a class of about 40 college students, most of them economics majors, whether the average student on campus would agree or disagree with a series of highly charged statements about selfishness and self-interest. Their answers were not reassuring. Sixty-five percent said that the average student would agree that "there is nothing more important to me than my own economic well-being," and 72 percent said that the typical student would agree that "I am not responsible for my neighbor." Seventy-five percent said their generation believed that "it's everyone for himself or herself in the American economy," and 88 percent said their fellow students would agree that "in our society everyone has to look out for number one." A stunning 96 percent thought their generation believed that "competition is the most important virtue in a market society," and 65 percent expected a typical student to agree that "people do not let moral scruples get in the way of their own advancement." In discussion, they explained that most students were apprehensive about their economic prospects, fearing that they would not do as well as their parents. If they wanted to succeed, they said, they would have to focus all their energies on "buttering their own bread."[14]

On the positive side, significantly lower percentages of the students, ranging from 30 to 50 percent, said that they personally subscribed to the selfish sentiments enumerated above. This is an indication that a significant sector of the younger generation remains committed to moral principles. My impression as a teacher is that a large percentage of today's college students remain generous and decent, although increasingly confused and torn between "making it" and remaining faithful to their moral ideals. Unfortunately, many sacrifice their intellectual loves to make big money, such as the student with a profound passion for the study of history who decided to give it up and become a corporate lawyer so that he could live the high life.

Growing student cynicism has led to an explosion of wilding on campuses across the country that started over a decade ago. A report by the Carnegie Foundation for the Advancement of Teaching released in 1990 found "a breakdown of civility and other disruptive forces" that are leaving campus life "in tatters." Of special concern is an epidemic of cheating, as well as a mushrooming number of racial attacks, rapes, and other hate crimes. Words, the currency of the university, are increasingly "used not as the key to understanding, but as weapons of assault."[15]

Campuses are no longer ivy-walled sanctuaries but increasingly have become sites of theft, sexual assault, property damage, and other crimes. The epidemic of alcoholism among students—70 percent qualify as binge drinkers at some colleges—has contributed to these rising crime rates. A study of 104 campuses conducted by the Harvard School of Public Health identified 44 colleges in which a majority of the students were binge drinkers. On these campuses, 9 out of 10 students said that they had suffered assaults, thefts, or other forms of violent intrusion, often by drunk students.[16]

Much campus crime, however, is committed sober by cold, calculating student wilders. A Harvard University student pleaded guilty in 1995 to stealing $6,838 raised at Harvard for the Jimmy Fund, a charity to help kids with cancer. Joann Plachy, a law student at Florida State University, was charged in 1995 with hiring a professional killer to murder a secretary who accused Plachy of having stolen a copy of an exam. In 2001 Joseph M. Mesa Jr., a 20-year-old freshman at Gallaudet University, reportedly confessed to killing two other students living in his dormitory, one four months after the other. He stabbed one classmate and fatally beat the other. His motive: petty robbery involving a few hundred dollars.[17]

The view of the campus as a haven from violent crime or other societal wilding is now as obsolete as the notion of the family itself as a safe haven. Ernest L. Boyer, the Carnegie Foundation's president, said that college promotional material "masks disturbing realities of student life" that mirror the "hard-edged competitive world" of the larger society.[18] Desperate for good grades, huge numbers of students routinely plagiarize papers and cheat on exams. Studies on many campuses, including Indiana University and the University of Tennessee, show that a majority of students admit to submitting papers written by others or copying large sections of friends' papers. A majority also confess to looking at other students' answers during in-class exams. "You could check for cheating in any class and you'd certainly find a significant portion of the people cheating," one M.I.T. student said, adding casually, "it's one way of getting through M.I.T."[19]

A controversy brewing in 2000 about fraudulent college admission essays shows that the cheating begins early in academic careers. Mothers, fathers, and other relatives often ghostwrite their kids' essays, and professional entrepreneurs are making entire careers off the new trend. Michele Hernandez, who used to work for admissions at Dartmouth, opened a dot-com that caters to applicants who need somebody to craft the admission essay for them. For $1,500, she will help write and polish the essay; if you come from a rich enough family, you can pay her $4,500 to complete your entire application.[20]

Technology, especially computers, has also made life easier for the new generation of student cheaters. Students routinely ask their friends for copies of old course papers on computer disk. It doesn't take much effort to rework a paper on a computer for a new class. One student at an elite Boston university said that nobody on campus thinks twice about the morality of such high-tech cheating. Students can buy online term papers about popular texts, including *The Wilding of America*.

Books on how to cheat are hot sellers on campus. Michael Moore, 24, has written a primer, *Cheating 101*, which has sold briskly on campuses around the country. He describes how to stuff crib sheets filled with useful facts into one's jeans or under one's baseball cap. He offers tips about how students can communicate answers on multiple-choice tests by shifting their feet under the desk in a prearranged code. About cheating, Moore says that "everyone's doing it" and that he's making an "honest living." About his decision to make an "honest living" by writing a how-to book on cheating, Moore says, "I'm just exercising my First Amendment rights."[21]

Although a significant minority of students are idealistic and intensely concerned about others, the majority appear to be increasingly cynical about their studies and their futures. They want to "invest as little time in their studies as possible," the Carnegie report suggests, while collecting their meal ticket and moving on to the professional gravy train. Fifty-five percent of faculty members complain that "most undergraduates . . . only do enough to get by." Carnegie Foundation president Boyer, however, noted that faculty are complicit in the problem by pursuing "their own research at the expense of teaching." He might have added that some faculty and administrators are the worst role models, as can be seen by looking at the growing faculty research scandal. In the 1990s, Congressman John Dingell uncovered science fraud in the biology labs of M.I.T. as well as unlawful diversion of research overhead expenditures for such things as "flowers, country-club memberships, and going-away parties for departing deans" in many of the nation's most famous universities, including Harvard, Stanford, and the California Institute of Technology. Stanford University president Donald Kennedy resigned after the media reported the extensive diversion of Stanford overhead funds to pay for such extravagances as a yacht. The reputation of Nobel laureate David Baltimore, one of the country's foremost cancer researchers and president of Rockefeller University, has been tarnished by the National Institutes of Health's conclusion that a member of Baltimore's own laboratory falsified data.[22]

In 2000 and 2001, controversies broke out about biotech and medical researchers making lucrative deals with pharmaceutical giants. This is just one sign of the growing presence of big corporations in university life. More professors are seeking equity stakes in companies or creating their own start-ups that give them a vested financial interest in how the data come out. As corporations fund bigger slices of academic research and the dot-com fever spreads among students, more professors sacrifice teaching quality and even research integrity to pursue their own fortunes. In February 2001, the dean of the Harvard Medical School ordered a broad review of the relations between the medical school and corporations funding research, including companies in which the university itself has equity. Dean Joseph Martin acknowledged that serious institutional bias may arise as universities and individual professors favor research linked to companies that can return the highest profit. Campus life breaks down as students, faculty, and administrators follow the narrow paths of their own careers and financial interests.[23]

All-American Drug Dealing: Unattainable Goals and Illegitimate Means

"I spend long hours, night and day, in crack houses and on drug-copping corners, observing, befriending, and interviewing street dealers, addicts, and anyone else who will pause to talk to me." Those are the words of anthropologist Philippe Bourgois, who spent five years living in an East Harlem tenement, although he was not looking to score a big drug deal; he was trying to get inside the minds of crack dealers to see what makes them tick. His conclusions are remarkable, suggesting that inner-city children bear a greater resemblance to careerist college students than anyone had imagined. Wilding at the bottom springs from the same basic recipe as wilding higher up.[24]

Bourgois describes a broken social world reminiscent of the Ik. Violence is everywhere, especially among people working or living with each other. Jackie was eight months pregnant when her crack-dealing husband, a drug lord of substantial means, was caught and sentenced to jail. Before he left, she shot him in the stomach in front of his associates. Instead of leaving her money before he was sent to prison, he had been squandering thousands on young women and "bragging about it."[25]

Jackie's violence so impressed the new drug lord that he hired her. At about the same time, Jackie started going with Julio, another dealer, who was being stalked by the lover of his ex-girlfriend, Rose, for refusing to pay for her abortion after he got her pregnant. Julio knew how to deal with violence, for he had been hired to guard a crack den where murderous stick-ups were common. On one occasion, Julio admitted "that he had been very nervous when robbers held a gun to his temple and asked for money and crack." Julio impressed his boss when he successfully hid some of the stash in a hollowed-out statue of a saint. But he did not tell his boss the whole truth. Julio "exaggerated to his boss the amount that had been stolen; he pocketed the difference himself."[26]

Julio had started out straight, working as a messenger for a magazine. There were no career possibilities for him there, and when he needed money to support a new crack habit, he realized he needed a better job fast. Like other crack dealers Bourgois got to know, Julio had become fed up with the "low wages and bad treatment" of the jobs available to him. He had bigger dreams of a career "offering superior wages and a dignified workplace," and he found it in the underground economy. After he started dealing crack, the money and new sense of "responsibility, success, and prestige" allowed him to kick his own crack habit.[27]

Bourgois concluded from his talks with Julio and other dealers that the view that

> the poor have been badly socialized and do not share mainstream values is wrong. On the contrary, ambitious, energetic inner-city youth are attracted to the underground [drug dealing] economy precisely because they believe in the rags-to-riches American Dream. Like many in the mainstream, they are frantically trying to get their piece of the pie as fast as possible.[28]

Drug dealers such as Julio, Bourgois finds, are meticulously following the "model for upward mobility" of the era, "aggressively setting themselves up as private entrepreneurs." Their dreams of wealth and success are precisely those of other youngsters tuned in to the glitter of television and videos. Rather than abandoning their dreams when the hard reality of their economic position sets in, they adopt an ambitious strategy consistent with the opportunities open to them.

Bourgois hints that it is hard to distinguish these street entrepreneurs from those in business schools and on Wall Street. They are equally dedicated to "making it" and equally ruthless in their business dealings. They are prepared to take unusual risks to realize their dream of fast money. The successful ones enjoy the same lifestyle, speeding "around in well-waxed Lincoln Continentals or Mercedes-Benzes." They invite friends and acquaintances "out to dinner in expensive restaurants almost every night." When a dealer parks his car on the street, "a bevy of attentive men and women . . . run to open the door for him."[29]

"Using the channels available," Bourgois writes, people such as Julio can be seen "as rugged individualists on an unpredictable frontier where fortune, fame, and destruction are all just around the corner." Widely presumed to be the archenemy of the American way of life, inner-city drug wilders are instead among the purest products of the American Dream.[30]

In 1995, William Adler published a book about ghetto children and drugs that conveys the same sad truth. Adler focused on the four Chambers brothers, originally from rural Arkansas, who moved to Detroit and built a gigantic cocaine business with all the trappings of a Fortune 100 corporation. The Chambers brothers were arrested and sent to jail, but not before they had created a conglomerate grossing at least $55 million—tax-free—a year.[31]

The Chambers story is not about inner-city youth as drug consumers, but as capitalists. The brothers promised their young employees, recruited from both cotton fields and the inner city, that they could get rich in a year, but only if they would give up their girlfriends and work hard. The crack company enforced strict discipline and work rules, offered health and benefit plans, performance bonuses, and quality improvement incentives. When the Chambers brothers were put in jail, other young crack entrepreneurs quickly took their place. After all, for thousands of inner-city youth, crack dealing is the only path to the American Dream.[32]

U.S. Business vs. Us

Global Capitalism and Corporate Wilding

*What do you mean **we**, kemo sabe?*

—Tonto to the Lone Ranger

A Fish Rots from the Head First

In January 2001, the U.S. Department of Labor reported that a clothing factory in American Samoa—a U.S. territory in the Pacific—producing for JCPenney, Sears, and Target was abusing hundreds of workers who were held as indentured servants. A Labor Department investigator said that many workers, who looked like "walking skeletons," lived "36 to a room and received bare-bones meals." The National Labor Committee, a New York–based public interest group, carried out its own detailed investigation, reporting that workers were beaten; sexually harassed; threatened with deportation; starved; forced to work 12- to 18-hour days, seven days a week; and made to live in rat-infested dormitories.[1]

On February 18, 2001, a report on the television program *60 Minutes* detailed some unseemly facts about the diamonds we associate with love and marriage. Brutal wars are fought in Zaire, Sierra Leone, the Congo, and other African countries to control access to the mines. *60 Minutes* focused on the role of giant corporations that allegedly help finance these wars, which are among the most brutal in recent memory (the Sierra Leone war is fought mainly by children whose fate when captured is to have their hands cut off). The *60 Minutes* report also explained why diamonds are so expensive; it is not because they are naturally scarce but because the largest companies exercise monopoly power to restrict supply and extract huge profits.

On May 10, 1993, a toy factory near Bangkok burned to the ground, killing 188 workers, mostly teenage girls. One surviving worker who jumped out of an upper-story window told investigators that she and some of the other workers had tried to escape down the stairs but had been commanded by supervisors to get back to work. Her sister also jumped, but died. The 188 deaths made this the worst industrial accident in history, exceeding the 146 garment workers killed in New York's Triangle Shirtwaist garment factory fire in 1911. But while the Triangle fire helped to inspire an era of regulatory reform, the tragedy in Thailand stands as a symbol of a new age of unregulated global wilding.

The Thai factory was owned by Kader Industrial Toy Company, a giant, global manufacturing conglomerate that contracts with Toys "R" Us, JCPenney, Fisher-Price, and other major American companies. *New York Times* columnist Bob Herbert wrote that the company had been running a sweatshop with young girls who were "semi-slave laborers." Calling it "terror in toyland," Herbert said that workers such as these girls slave for "grotesquely low wages and in disgusting and extremely dangerous conditions."[2]

We have focused thus far on wilding by individuals, but wilding by corporations and governments plays a huge role in our growing crisis. Such wilding, as discussed in Chapter 1, involves behavior by institutions that enhance their own wealth and power by harming workers, citizens, and communities. Our new wilding crisis—in the United States and increasingly in the world at large—is fueled by the predatory behavior of multinational firms that seek fast profits at any price. Such corporations collude with governments and are driven both by the financial markets and by unfettered greed.

This chapter's focus on corporate wilding helps make clear that wilding starts from the top. The leaders of giant corporations and their political and intellectual allies are at the heart of the wilding crisis. They create the institutional conditions and reigning ideologies that catalyze wilding at all levels of society.

A thin line has always divided the capitalist quest for profit from economic wilding. John D. Rockefeller, Andrew Carnegie, and the other robber barons of the late nineteenth century who built American capitalism were spectacular economic wilders, famous for their brutal treatment of workers and corrupt, monopolistic practices. In the famous 1893 Homestead Steel strike, Carnegie ordered his workers shot. Since then, we have suffered repeated cycles of wilding—the Roaring Twenties, with its huge speculative binges and political scandals, for example—that have chipped away at the nation's moral fabric.

The tenuous line between business success and wilding is being even more dangerously blurred by two fundamental changes. The first is the institutionalization of the radically individualistic political economy ushered in during the 1980s and championed now by President George W. Bush. The Reagan revolution enshrined a new free-market religion, worshiping business and profits and demonizing labor unions and government. It has become the dominant ideology of our times and is fanning the flames of wilding from Wall Street to Main Street.

The second change is the rise of global capitalism, the most fundamental economic shift of our times. The new global system threatens to destroy the social dikes against corporate wilding that national governments, labor organizations, and communities have struggled to build throughout the last two centuries of the Industrial Revolution.

Capitalism vs. Community: Sociological Prophets and Global Profits

The making of a global economy is the real business of the twenty-first century. Huge multinational companies are spreading their wings for global flight, capitalizing on technological and communications revolutions to produce and market their wares from the Amazon to the Pacific Basin. Wall Street is eagerly financing the new global system, helping create the financial markets that send trillions of dollars across the globe every day at lightning speed. Meanwhile, America's political leaders, both Republican and Democratic, are sponsoring a torrent of free-trade treaties, from the North American Free Trade Agreement (NAFTA) and the Free Trade for Africa Agreement to the proposed new Free Trade Agreement of the Americas. The World Trade Organization—the target of the turbulent 1999 Seattle protests—is laying the legal groundwork for a new economic world order.

Globalization is being created by a new "corpocracy"—a worldwide nexus of financial markets and corporations that now dominates the world. There are more than 45,000 corporations in the world today, but the 200 largest companies rule, with sales comprising more than 25 percent of the world's total gross domestic product (GDP). Financial institutions are especially important, with the 100 largest banks controlling $21 trillion in assets, about three-fourths of the world's wealth. The biggest companies, such as Citigroup, General Electric (GE), and General Motors (GM), are global empires with no national loyalty. They are larger and more powerful than most countries; GM's annual sales are greater than the entire GDP of Poland; Wal-Mart's are greater than the GDP of Israel or Denmark.[3]

The rush toward a global economy is the most revolutionary development of our times. It has the potential to bring many benefits, including a more robust world economy, dynamic growth in corners of the world that have known only poverty and despair, and even the development of a new world community. But in its current form, it threatens to pit the interests of businesses against those of their host societies, creating a new predatory capitalism based on worldwide economic wilding.

Concepts developed a century ago by the founders of sociology are powerful tools for understanding this new wilding threat. As we saw in Chapter 1, the great French sociologist Émile Durkheim argued that early industrial capitalism, by destroying traditional communities and encouraging individual ambition and mobility, endangered social solidarity and the survival of society itself. The burgeoning industrial era bred a culture of egoism and anomie—egoism reflecting the loss of community and anomie, the rise of socially unregulated dreams and passions. Egoism and anomie are fertile breeding grounds for wilding, spawning self-interest, greed, and violence that can spiral out of control and subvert society.

Globalism promises to further weaken the social ties and values that civilize both individuals and business. Unencumbered by national loyalties, corporations now roam the world searching for the cheapest labor in desperately poor countries. As U.S. corporations move overseas, U.S. communities themselves become more vulnerable, with shuttered plants and industrial ghost towns becoming fixtures of the American landscape. Thrown into competition with workers in developing countries, millions of U.S. workers face an uncertain future, and many become "temps," unable to find steady, full-time employment. In the words of some observers, the multinational corporation is itself becoming a virtual, or hollow, community, with transient "contractors" replacing permanent employees. This erosion of community intensifies both egoism and anomie, transforming growing numbers of employees into rootless, atomized "entrepreneurs," constantly seeking reemployment. At the same time, the multinationals and their top managers are increasingly liberated from governmental regulation, free to pursue unbounded appetites for global power and vast worldwide profits.

Although the twentieth century proved Karl Marx's predictions about capitalism's death to be folly, globalism eerily vindicates Marx's view of the potential for capitalist wilding. The market's function of reducing all behavior to the cash nexus and naked self-interest becomes increasingly relevant in a global economy. Employees who must act as entrepreneurs find no shelter from the market and survive only by embracing relentless self-promotion. Major American corporations, seeking bonanza profits, pursue child labor in India and prison labor in China.

Marx recognized that the great moral problem of capitalism is the incentive of business to make money by exploiting its employees. In a global economy, this problem assumes a new scale. The core of the current wilding threat arises from the intensification of appetites whetted by the new fantastic global possibilities and from the ingenious new multinational corporate strategies for realizing them.

The Musical Chairs of Global Business: The New Corporate Wilding

The key is a game of global musical chairs—a master strategy for maximizing profits by pitting national workforces against one another and exploiting the immense leverage of capital flight. Corporations able to hire cheap labor around the world can threaten to leave a community unless workers submit to lower pay or local governments agree to various incentives to keep companies from pulling up stakes. Such intimidation has also been one of business's trump cards, played 50 years ago by Massachusetts and New Hampshire textile mill owners, for example, who relocated from New England to the South after northern workers unionized. But musical chairs becomes a game plan for unparalleled wilding when the theater shifts from the nation-state to the world—and the mill owners can relocate to South Korea or Mexico.

Here, the analyses of Durkheim and Marx converge. Musical chairs in the national arena has been a regulated game, with national governments playing the role of arbiter and community protector of last resort. Such national regulation restricts the degree of egoism and anomie that can arise from the economic game and limits exploitation by prohibiting child labor, enforcing minimum wages, and protecting the environment. Within U.S. national capitalism, labor agreements and government programs created during and after the 1930s New Deal era helped to ensure that higher profits for companies translated into higher wages for their workers and more resources for their host communities. This linking of corporate and community interests lent some credibility to the corporate manifesto expressed in the 1950s by the president of General Motors: "What's good for GM is good for America."

Under global capitalism today, however, there is no effective regulatory watchdog for the world community. As an unregulated game, global musical chairs opens societies all over the world to a purely egoistic and anomic world economy. The danger is that such a game veers, as we shall see in the rest of this chapter, toward new rules that allow businesses to maximize profit by undermining the health of their host societies. As the global economy regresses back to the raw capitalism of an earlier era, the social protections built up over two centuries are jeopardized.

Global economic wilding is the fruit of active collaboration between multinational companies and national governments. Markets, whether national or global, are always shaped by those with power, and while it may seem strange that national governments would collaborate in their own demise, they have, during the last two decades, played a major role in subverting their own authority as they help write the rules of the new global game. This collaboration reflects incestuous entanglements among multinationals and political elites in both developed and developing countries who have struck deals that too often subvert their own societies. These deals have triggered a downward competitive spiral—a "race to the bottom," as some global observers have dubbed it—among economies around the world, pushing much of America toward third world wages and working conditions while intensifying the misery of already impoverished masses in poor countries.[4]

Wilding around the World: The Third World as Global Sweatshop

On the campus where I teach, a Vietnam-style revolt is mushrooming. Students are outraged about Boston College caps and sweatshirts allegedly being made in sweatshops in Indonesia, Mexico, and El Salvador. As my students push the university to stop using sweatshop products, similar protests have spread like wildfire across many other campuses throughout the country. Sweatshops have become the symbol of the economic wilding at the heart of the new global economy.

Some students may have read about the famous Gilded Age journalist Upton Sinclair, who ventured into the terrifying meat factories of Chicago. In his classic book, *The Jungle*, published in 1906, he described a world of 16-hour workdays paying pennies per hour in slaughterhouses producing poisoned meat rotting with blood and hair. A century later, Sinclair's graphic sketch of the sweatshop economy still scorches the brain and shapes our understanding of economic wilding of an earlier age.

The Upton Sinclair of today's global economy is Charles Kernaghan, the New York–based muckraker most famous for his exposure of sweatshops in El Salvador making clothes for Kathie Lee Gifford's clothing line. Kathie Lee claims to have broken down in tears when she listened to Salvadoran workers who stitched the clothes bearing her label. Most workers were young girls aged 14 to 24, and they outlined their 20-hour shifts from 6:50 A.M. to 3:00 A.M. the next morning, with one 40-minute break in the day at noon for lunch. The girls described death threats for attempted unionizing, mandatory pregnancy tests, forced overtime, and starvation wages of 60 cents an hour. Managers refused to let them get up or move from their worksites, or to permit more than two daily bathroom visits. The girls also told of bosses cursing and yelling at them to sew faster and exceed the madcap production norm of 100 to 150 pieces an hour. Their plants are behind barbed wire and look like prisons.

Ground zero of the global workshop is China, with its 1 billion–plus workers. In 2000, after numerous trips to Chinese factories, Kernaghan wrote: "When you see an Ann Taylor suit on sale for $198, do you ever imagine 20-year-old women in China being forced to work 96 hours a week, from 7 A.M. to midnight, seven days a week, and being paid just 14 cents an hour? When you think of Ralph Lauren or Ellen Tracy, do you imagine women in China being paid 23 cents an hour to work 15 hour shifts six days a week?" Global companies, he writes, "are actually lowering standards in China, slashing wages and benefits, extending forced overtime hours, and weakening respect for human rights while relocating their work to a growing sector of unregulated foreign-owned sweatshops in the south of China."[5]

Similar conditions of workplace wilding prevail in Central America in places such as the Chentex plant in the Las Mercedes Free-Trade Zone in Nicaragua that makes blue jeans for Kohl's, Target, JCPenney, and other leading U.S. companies, as well as uniforms for the U.S. military, their biggest client. The base pay at the Chentex plant is 19 cents an hour. When workers asked for an 8-cent wage increase, Chentex fired the entire union leadership, had many organizers arrested, and built new barbed-wire fences. Conditions inside the plant are a nightmare. Managers scream and harass workers constantly to force them to work faster and longer. A 21-year-old worker, Sanchez, says, "They yelled at us, kicked us, hit us in the face or buttocks, and pulled our ears." Two members of the U.S. House of Representatives who went to see for themselves were outraged by the sweatshop conditions and the fact that U.S. taxpayers were indirectly footing the bill through the Pentagon procurements. After returning from Nicaragua, where they talked to workers, Congresswoman Sherrod Brown wrote in February 2001, "I have joined with Congresswoman Cynthia McKinney, Democrat of Georgia, a member of the Military Procurement Subcommittee, in requesting that the General Accounting Office investigate the Pentagon's role in this sweatshop. We will not sit quietly as members of the Army and Air Force support sweatshops in Nicaragua."[6]

Most developing countries have established special "export processing zones" or "free-trade zones" that offer "tax holidays" to multinationals and exempt them from environmental codes and labor laws. Sometimes walled off behind barbed-wire fences, these zones—where corporations locate their sweatshops and get state protection for every manner of economic wilding—have been described as "huge labor camp[s]," often controlled by special police forces. The most famous of these zones, and among the most important to American companies, is along the U.S.–Mexican border, which is the site of the *maquiladora* plants that now reach well into the Mexican interior.[7]

Growing out of the Border Industrialization Program of 1965, the *maquiladoras* are a classic instance of collaboration between multinationals and government. The Mexican government offered corporations favorable land deals, waived custom clearance and import duties, and agreed to low taxes and, tacitly, the right to run their businesses with a free hand, exempt from environmental and labor laws. The U.S. government did its share by running political interference for U.S. companies and giving them technical assistance and tax breaks for going south of the border. The passage of NAFTA in 1993 facilitated the huge American corporate exodus to south of the border, swelling the ranks of displaced Mexican workers in agriculture and other industries that cannot survive American competition. Today, there are more than 40,000 foreign factories and more than 4,000 U.S. plants in Mexico, including Fortune 500 giants such as GM, Nike, and GE.[8]

The case of the Kukdong factory in Atlixco, Mexico, which produces sweatshirts and other collegiate apparel for Nike, suggests that sweatshops remain the norm rather than the exception. In early 2001, investigations by the International Labor Rights Fund and the Worker Rights Consortium found that the Kukdong plant is a huge corporate wilder.

Kukdong supervisors physically and verbally abuse employees. The factory refuses to pay legally mandated sick pay and maternity benefits, denies workers five hours' wages each week, forces workers to eat in a plant cafeteria where food is spoiled and worm-infested, and imposes a company union while beating and firing workers seeking to organize an independent union.[9]

Mexican labor lawyers who have independently investigated the Kukdong factory concluded that the failure to reinstate striking workers fighting for an independent union is the central issue. At Chentex, Kukdong, and other plants in free-trade zones across the world, employers are waging a war over this issue because they realize that such unions are the only tools workers now have to combat corporate wilding. The courage of the organizers and strikers in risking their jobs and lives has brought international attention to the issue and forced companies such as Nike to order its own independent investigation of Kukdong.

The absence of unions has meant a continued slide in Mexican wages and working conditions. In October 2000, Oscar Chavez Diaz, an Alcoa employee in Acuna, Mexico, showed a *New York Times* reporter a weekly pay stub for $60. Diaz lives with his wife in the rusting shell of a school bus and says he lacks money for food and clothing. Ruth Rosenbaum, a social economist who has recently concluded a study of the purchasing power of 11 border communities, says the misery is getting worse: "You study these wages for a while," she says, "and it makes you sick to your stomach." Another assembly-line employee at Alcoa, Isidro Esquivel Sanchez, said, "They work us like donkeys, and we come back to this" as he pointed to his one-room, dirt-floor hovel. According to the *Times* reporter, "In Acuna, as in other border settlements, Mexican workers earn such miserable wages and American companies pay such minimal taxes that its schools are a shambles, its hospital crumbling, its trash collection slapdash and sewage lines collapsed." More than 50 percent of the border workers have no indoor bathroom.[10]

Alcoa is a highly profitable company chaired until recently by Paul O'Neill, who was George W. Bush's Secretary of the Treasury from 2001 to 2002. He presided over Alcoa during some of its worst abuses of worker rights in Mexico. In his role as Treasury Secretary O'Neill was a central player in shaping U.S. trade policy with Mexico, which emphasizes, as it has all over the world, enforcement of property rights and bailouts of rich investors while dismissing labor rights and environmental standards.

Another very serious form of global economic wilding, long visible in the *maquiladoras*, is the sexual abuse of young female workers. Young women between 14 and 26 make up more than two-thirds of the work-

force in most free-trade zones. Labor lawyers and social workers in the *maquiladoras* report that young women are often propositioned by their male supervisors and can lose their jobs if they don't sleep with them. Mexican social worker Teresa Almada reports that women are in "a lot of danger," both inside and outside the factory gates, and that many become pregnant and are then fired.[11]

Corporate wilding also includes massive environmental abuse. *Maquiladoras* have dumped millions of tons of raw sewage into rivers, many flowing up into the United States. A study by the AFL-CIO found the water supply on the border to be massively polluted; indiscriminate dumping of toxic waste in unsafe, often clandestine, dump sites threatens fish and wildlife with extinction and the ecosystem as a whole.[12]

In addition, workers are subjected to toxic conditions inside the plants. Anthropologist Maria Fernandez-Kelly, who worked in the plants in Ciudad Juarez, reports that workers' health tends to deteriorate rapidly because of the brutal work pace, unsafe machinery, and hazardous fumes, with the most frequent complaints being "eyesight deterioration, and nervous and respiratory ailments." A survey conducted by the University of Massachusetts at Lowell found widespread musculoskeletal disorders related to the pace of work and poor workplace engineering. Many studies have found serious health problems caused by toxic chemicals and other unregulated pollution.[13]

Foreign companies are producing wealth and a booming border economy, but most of the wealth flows back into the corporations' own coffers. Gustavo Elizondo, the mayor of Juarez, says that the sad reality of his community is that it is "a place of opportunity for the international community" but has left the local government unable "to provide water, sewage and sanitation." According to the 2000 Mexican census, 75 percent of Mexicans live in poverty today, compared with 49 percent in 1981. "Every year we get poorer and poorer," the Juarez mayor concludes, "even though we create more and more wealth."[14]

The prevailing subhuman conditions in the plants and the surrounding communities are a product of coordinated repression by multinational corporations and the Mexican government, which has intervened repeatedly, using the police and the army to suppress labor protests and permitting multinational companies to evade environmental and labor laws. Wages and working conditions have declined as the multinationals have expanded because the huge firms have worked so effectively with the U.S. and Mexican governments and with company-sponsored unions to erode workers' rights and community social protections. These are neither free nor fair markets, but rather the predictable outcome of a global game of musical chairs gone wild.

Globalization without Wilding: The Future of Globalization after the Battle of Seattle

In December 1999, the streets of Seattle became a fiery battleground with U.S. tanks on the streets, Nike windows shattered, and tear gas shots heard around the world. Fifty thousand protesters—many of them college students teaming up with workers and environmentalists ("Teamsters for Turtles")—rallied to shut down the meeting of the World Trade Organization (WTO). Their goal was not to end globalization but to challenge the WTO—which helps make the rules of the global economy—to make new regulations protecting human rights as well as protecting money.[15]

Seattle was a Constitutional Moment, a recognition that financial elites from the richest nations are making basic rules that will determine how the world is run for decades to come. The protesters, who want globalization without wilding, have shown their determination; they have mounted electrifying protests since Seattle at nearly every meeting of the financial elites who make the rules. As the corporate elites look for places to meet in quiet secrecy (choosing in 2001 to hold the WTO meeting in the Mideast dictatorship desert of Quatar), the protesters defy efforts to be deterred by police violence and armed fortifications. At the 2001 meeting of the World Economic Forum, in Davos, Switzerland, many protesters actually skied in to evade blockades at the border and on the streets.

As noted at the beginning of this chapter, globalization could be organized in a different way to reap the benefits of global specialization, production, and trade without inflicting harm on millions of the world's workers and communities. Why, then, have our political leaders allowed globalization to proceed in its current form? And how might the global economy be restructured and regulated to balance the enormous power of multinational corporations and contain their greed?

The United States will retain significant influence in the web of global institutions, from the International Monetary Fund (IMF) and the World Bank to the World Trade Association. But the players gaining the most power in the new world economy are not governments, but the multinationals themselves. The reason both Republican and Democratic presidents acquiesce to the multinationals' agenda is simple: Both political parties are dependent upon business funding to win elections and are not prepared to risk opposing huge global corporations on issues of central importance to them. Five hundred of the largest U.S. corporations have offices in Washington and employ thousands of lobbyists, as do 400 of the largest foreign multinationals. Together, these corporations constitute by far the largest and most influential special-interest group in Washington. Ultimately, business sets the parameters for economic policymaking in America because of their lobbying efforts and because members of the U.S. corporate elite themselves occupy the highest governmental economic posts, thereby controlling the money and investment decisions essential to the survival of both the population and the government.[16]

Students and other Seattle protesters have already shown that their actions can force change. The protests in 2000 and 2001 triggered a major crisis among the financial elites, with corporations rushing to embrace an image of social responsibility. The president of the World Bank, James Wolfensohn, claims that he is now moving his agency to focus on the needs of the global poor. The U.S. government has pulled back some of its support for institutions such as the IMF and has indicated a concern with introducing labor and environmental rights in trade agreements.

The aim of the protesters is to turn globalization into a means of empowering people and dignifying their lives. One approach is to promote global labor movements to represent the interests of the new global workforce and balance the power of the multinationals. Both American workers and employees in developing nations need strong unions to prevent the horrendous exploitation of global sweatshops and contingent employment. But the U.S. government has avoided any identification with American unions and has done nothing to support the embryonic movement for independent unions in Mexico, Indonesia, and other developing countries. President George W. Bush, with his long anti-labor record, has abandoned even the small steps that President Clinton took to promote unions and labor rights around the world, which included the effort to introduce provisions for worker and environmental rights into NAFTA and at WTO negotiations.

American unions are starting to develop new international strategies. U.S. unions now realize that when we allow corporations to operate sweatshops abroad, foreign workers will begin to encounter sweatshop conditions at home. After years of hostility to foreign workers and foreign labor movements, the AFL-CIO labor chiefs have begun to speak about international labor solidarity and to put their money where their mouths are. John Sweeney, current president of the AFL-CIO, has provided vocal support and funding for organizing efforts in the *maquiladoras* and other trade zones. As early as 1994, workers in a Ford truck-assembly plant in St. Paul, Minnesota, voted to send funds to Ford workers in Mexico to support a union drive in the *maquiladoras*. The American workers, who recognized that wretched Mexican wages and working conditions affected their own jobs and security, wore patches on their jackets saying "Cross-Border Solidarity Organizers." A growing number of labor unions—such as the U.S. United Electrical Workers, with help from the Teamsters—have begun to contribute to independent labor organizing in the *maquiladoras*.[17]

The rise of new international labor confederations—in coalition with student groups, environmentalists, and other human rights groups—could help prevent multinationals from playing one country's workers against another's in a race to the bottom. It could also help create new controls over the unchecked lightning-fast movement of speculative capital around the planet. As the Asian crisis of 1998 showed, such fast money can easily destabilize the economies of entire continents and erode the ability of nations to protect their own people. We need foreign investment and trade, but only when there are speed bumps and checks that allow nations and communities to control their own destinies.[18]

Ultimately, a new democratic coalition must become a major player at the tables where the new constitution of the global economy is being written. The finance ministers of the rich nations and the corporate advisory teams who meet regularly at the WTO, IMF, and World Bank will have to make room for a whole new set of worker and citizen representatives. Global rules will have to shift from their exclusive focus on protecting property rights and free trade. The new mission is to create a democratic model of globalization, centered on respect for human rights and a fair distribution of wealth between rich and poor nations, as well as between corporate CEOs and their global workforce.[19]

This may seem a long, steep climb, but one immediate step along the way is to build codes of international labor standards and corporate conduct that would set a humane global floor for wages and working conditions. The European Union has established a European Social Charter that sets minimum wages, health and safety standards, and other social codes to be honored by all the member nations. The International Labor Organization (ILO) has a code of global labor rights that now needs to be toughened and enforced in all nations and corporations, with sanctions imposed on companies that wild by ignoring the codes. Although President Clinton negotiated NAFTA with side agreements to protect labor and the environment, most observers saw them as pitifully weak. Citizen and labor groups are pushing for far stronger agreements that are consistent with or stronger than current United Nations and ILO standards, and for a robust social charter for *maquiladora* businesses.[20]

Apparel companies such as Nike, Reebok, and Wal-Mart have banded together in the Fair Labor Association to form their own corporate codes of conduct, promising to avoid use of child labor or prison labor and to pay the prevailing wages in each country in which they operate. Such corporate codes across an entire sector are an important first step to end corporate wilding. But it will take public action to make the companies accountable and truly end the new wave of global economic wilding. Students in the anti-sweatshop movement have proved that even huge, ruthless companies such as Nike can be forced to change by consumer boycotts. Across the nation, students have become more careful about their own buying habits and mounted visible boycotts at Nike stores that helped change Nike policy. They also forced their universities to break ties with companies that operated sweatshops around the world, and have helped create new monitoring and enforcement agencies to ensure that the companies do not continue to wild on the sly.[21]

Multinational companies in the United States and elsewhere have used globalism to escape their social responsibilities and weaken the accountability that the workers and governments of their own nations have historically imposed on them. This will lead to a permanent regime of corporate wilding unless a new social covenant is negotiated between multinationals and the workers and citizens of the world. Building a new world community through the struggle for global employee rights and democratic and accountable multinational corporations may prove the most important new social movement of the coming era.

5

Enron

Systemic Wilding in the Corridors of Power

The Enron drama in 2001 was one of the great business scandals of the modern era. This was not simply because Enron was the seventh-largest American corporation, nor because an even bigger company, the telecom giant WorldCom, went bust a few months later and became the biggest bankruptcy in history. Nor was it because 570 other corporations were accused of corporate fraud in 2002, constituting one of the largest corporate crime waves in history. Rather, Enron was important precisely because so much of the wilding it represented was perfectly legal and because it involved not only huge corporations but Wall Street, the accounting and legal professions, and much of Washington D.C. It was a crisis that undermined public faith in the integrity of the market system, suggesting that a systemic wilding event was shaking the capitalist order and opening up the possibility of unforeseen change in the system itself.

In this chapter, we consider the meaning of systemic wilding, which goes beyond the wilding of particular individuals or even of specific institutions. President George W. Bush framed the crisis as the wilding of a few corporate executives. He said that there are always a few "bad apples" and that the executives who committed crimes at Enron, WorldCom, and other companies would be aggressively prosecuted. But as the crisis unfolded, it became clear that this was not just about a few "bad apples" or even the specific companies they directed. This was a case of the barrel itself being rotten, infecting nearly all the apples in one way or another. If a few "bad apples" is a metaphor for individual wilding or the wilding of a small number of companies, a rotten barrel evokes the meaning of systemic wilding, which can only be fixed by constructing a new barrel.

Systemic wilding is the wilding that emerges from a set of corrupted intertwined institutions at the core of our economic and political order. While presumably acting as checks and balances or watchdogs on each others' conduct, these institutions are increasingly melded together into a monolith of power that inflicts severe harm on ordinary people as it siphons wealth to the elites it represents. The only solution to systemic wilding is systemic change. Here, we use the Enron crisis to look at the major institutional players who collaborate to create systemic wilding and to show the new forms of accountability that will be required to make things right.

Enron and Systemic Wilding

The whistle-blower at Enron who blew open the entire scandal was an unlikely hero. Sherron Watkins, a 40-something accountant and a devoted Enron employee, told a rapt congressional panel about going to her boss, founder and chairman of Enron, Kenneth Lay, and telling him point-blank that Enron was on the brink of financial disaster because of deceptive accounting practices. Watkins testified that she told Lay that the chief financial officers of the company, including CEO Jeffrey Skilling and CFO Andrew Fastow, had concocted a shadowy network of Enron-funded off-book financial entities that were shielding massive and growing Enron debt. If the process continued, Watkins warned, Enron would quickly descend into insolvency and might face serious legal liability. The mysterious special financial entities, with bizarre names such as Chewko, Raptor, LJM Cayman, and LJM 2, were allegedly being used by Skilling and Fastow to skim off big money (Fastow made more than $45 million from the LJMs alone). Chewko, Raptor, and the LJMs also cleverly fogged the view of investors, workers, and the public about Enron's increasingly desperate financial situation. Ken Lay dithered and Enron's board of directors dallied, later pleading ignorance but essentially underwriting the orgy of deception and fraud.

Enron was a company used to big profits. Within ten years, Enron transformed itself from a small, stodgy energy business into a "new economy" financial company that gambled on global energy trades and acquisitions. The ethos of fast money and high living attracted executives such as Fastow, whom a high school teacher once called a "budding wheeler-dealer." Fastow was known at Enron as "an intimidating and single-minded self-promotor," embodying the Enron culture of "me first, I want to get paid."[1]

As Enron got deeper into the speculative world of trading, its executives saw themselves as a special breed. They gambled on high stakes with happy abandon and strategies "close to the edge." The *Wall Street Journal* reported that the prevailing corporate culture was "to push everything to the limits: business practices, laws and personal behavior."[2] Enron executives showed off by paying over $5,000 for choice company parking spots; they spent money on expensive Porsches and celebrated lucky deals by going down to local strip clubs and throwing lots of money on the table. *Fortune* magazine reported that a dancer at the Treasures strip joint said that a group of Enron execs marched in after one deal and announced that they had $10,000 to spend on the best girls.[3]

The debt deception and profit skimming by executives was just one component of the web of wilding engulfing Enron. An Enron executive pled guilty to conspiracy to drive up prices in secret and illegal energy deals orchestrated by Enron in California that led to disastrous electric power shortages, blackouts, and massively inflated prices for California consumers. Enron engaged in similar extortionary energy trading practices in Britain and around the world, going abroad to reap tax advantages and government subsidies while concealing debt. Enron's power plant operations in India and its proposed pipeline operations in Bolivia both exploited political connections—in India to crack down on dissent from workers and in Bolivia to silence local communities concerned for their environments. In what created the most public outrage, Enron locked its workers into pension funds invested exclusively in Enron stock even as the executives were selling off their own Enron shares and cashing in their stock options, knowing that the stock would collapse soon and leave many of their workers without a penny for their retirement. Thousands of workers were devastated by this loss.

In the heady world of the dot-com economy and the 1990s market bubble, scores of big companies plunged headlong into their own "creative accounting." Driven by greed and the new relentless demands for higher earnings on Wall Street, executives at WorldCom, Qwest, Global Crossing, Imclone, Kmart, Adelphi, Tyco, Cendant, and Martha Stewart Enterprises have all been indicted for fraud, inside dealing, or similar charges. The intense Wall Street pressure on the companies for big profits and soaring stock prices does not justify corporate deceptive conduct, but it does point to the systemic character of the wilding and explain the spread of the crisis across the entire economy. Numerous other companies, notably Harken Energy, the company on whose board George W. Bush served as a director, and Halliburton, the energy firm once run by Dick Cheney, all came under investigation for allegedly hiding debt, inflating profits, or pulling insider sweetheart deals for top executives, many paying the CEOs unconscionable options and bonuses as the ship was going down.

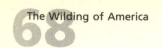

Arthur Andersen: Master of Unaccountable Accounting

The accounting profession may not seem glamorous, but the green eye-shaders are vital to the integrity of the market system. They are essential watchdogs who vouch for the honesty of financial reporting and help to sustain faith in the markets. By partnering with Enron to create its deception and fraud, the accountants (along with the bankers, lawyers, and politicians) helped transform one company's wilding into the nightmare of systemic wilding.

Arthur Andersen was one of the Big 5, the great accounting firms who audit the Fortune 500 companies and put the Good Housekeeping seal of approval on their financial statements. But only months after the Enron scandal broke, Arthur Andersen became the symbol of accounting gone wild. Andersen had been the auditor not only for Enron, but for WorldCom and many of the other firms that have been investigated for "misstatements," including Cheney's Halliburton. Cheney had made a video testifying to Andersen's integrity which would come back to haunt him.

Andersen became a key target of Justice Department investigations and was indicted for numerous violations, including obstruction of justice for shredding Enron-related material. A Houston jury that convicted Andersen of obstruction watched a video in which an Andersen manager tells the Enron audit team that destroying documents even the day before the litigation is "great" because anything useful to the courts was gone. David Duncan, the chief Andersen accountant on the Enron audit team, confessed that he personally destroyed documents and testified that, just before the trial, Andersen employees worked overtime to delete hundreds of computer files and shred "tons" of documents, in the process overloading the shredding machines and causing them to malfunction.[4]

While Andersen top executives continued to maintain that they had nothing to hide, the shredding hinted that Andersen was up to its eye-shades in Enron's financial fraud, helping craft the infamous special partnerships and signing off on statements affirming their legality. Governments and creditors have filed numerous suits against Andersen to punish it for fraud and to redeem Enron-related losses. Texas revoked Andersen's license and the Justice Department filed its first major criminal charge in the Enron case against Andersen for covering up and destroying documents and e-mails.

Andersen CEO Joseph Berardino admitted that "what was done was not in keeping with the values and heritage of this firm. It was wrong." But Berardino said that only a few Andersen employees had erred.[5]

The problem was a systemic conflict of interest between truthful accounting and making money. Accounting firms have become not only auditors but consultants, making fortunes off their new expansive roles. Had Andersen not played ball with Fastow and Skilling, signing off on the deceptive Chewko, Raptor, and LJM entities, Enron would have found another accounting firm willing to play the game. To blow the whistle in their auditing role would have not only jeopardized their fees as accountants but forfeited the millions Andersen made in its other role as consultant to Enron. Andersen symbolized the structural conflict of interest that threatens the integrity of all of today's green eyeshaders.

Merrill Lynch and Wilding on Wall Street

The Enron crisis could not have occurred without the complicity of the biggest players on Wall Street. Their role is critical to understanding systemic wilding, since the big banks lie at the center of the capitalist system. The investment banks' relations to Enron and other corporate clients have become clouded with conflicts of interest—sometimes criminal but mostly legal—a hint of wilding that is integral to the system itself.

On July 28, 2003, J. P. Morgan Chase and Citibank agreed to pay $300 million in fines for helping Enron misrepresent its financial condition. The banks advised Enron on structuring its off-the-books partnerships that deceptively inflated earnings and concealed debt. In February 2003, the SEC fined Merrill Lynch $80 million for two transactions also involving Enron's secret partnerships. The SEC also charged four Merrill executives with aiding and abetting fraud related to a sham 1999 Enron deal involving LJM2, a key Fastow partnership, in which 100 Merrill employees personally invested funds.[6] Several British bankers, including three at Greenwich NatWest bank, have also been indicted for Enron-related fraud.[7]

Why would banks get involved in financing and marketing off-book schemes that might be used for concealing debts or inflating profits? By doing so, the banks consolidated a web of profitable relationships with Enron and other companies, enriching themselves by helping the companies enrich themselves.[8] According to a 2002 class action suit filed by Enron shareholders (led by chief claimant University of California and still being litigated at this writing), Merrill Lynch, Citigroup, and J.P. Morgan Chase not only helped design Enron's debt-concealing entities, but invested heavily in them and profited from the deceptive accounting schemes. Merrill Lynch allegedly raised $390 million for LJM2 and invested $40 million in another Enron secret entity called Zephyrus. As determined by the SEC in its Merrill Lynch settlement and alleged by Enron bankruptcy examiner, attorney Neal Batson, in a February 14, 2003, court report, these big banks that invested in Enron stock were involved in deals that concealed debt from investors and made money off of Enron's soaring reputation and stock prices, inflated by the Raptors, LJMs, and other secret partnerships, as well as by the misleading and optimistic reports of analysts employed by the banks themselves. Batson's report, which is thicker than the Manhattan phone book and is known as the St. Valentine's Day Massacre, is the first of two bankruptcy reports alleging grounds for indicting Wall Street bankers who were in bed with Enron executives, quite literally in the case of one fired Texas-based Merrill Lynch banker, Schuyler Tilney, whose wife, Elizabeth, was an Enron marketing executive known for inventing Enron's infamous crooked E logo. Schuyler Tilney is one of the four Merrill Lynch executives already charged by the SEC for aiding Enron fraud.[9]

On April 28, 2003, a Senate governmental affairs subcommitee accused Merrill Lynch of helping concoct a 1999 sham deal relating to the sale of Nigerian barges that inflated Enron's profits by $12 million, a deceptive Fastow LJM2 deal that is also the basis for the SEC charges against the four Merrill Lynch bankers. On another matter, the subcommittee found that when Enron threatened to cancel business with Merrill Lynch after a negative Merrill Lynch analyst report, Merrill Lynch replaced the analyst with a new one who promptly upgraded Enron stock, leading Enron to award Merrill Lynch more than $2.5 billion in new underwriting business. Senator Peter Fitzgerald (R-Ill) concluded that "it's clear that Merrill Lynch has been investment banker to a big Ponzi Scheme."[10]

As a team of *Frontline* investigators summarized it, the big investment banks tied to Enron "were involved in designing the structure of these hidden partnerships, and then made money from investing in them." The banks' profits from Enron stock soared along with the stock price itself, inflated by the fraudulent partnerships and analysts' "buy ratings." The banks simultaneously profited from lucrative underwriting fees that were part of their intertwined, multifaceted relation with Enron.[11]

The Wall Street analysts' conflict of interest has become one of the biggest Enron-related stories. Like the accountants, Wall Street analysts play a vital role in sustaining faith in the integrity of the market system, with their research on companies presumed to be "objective" and their buy and sell recommendations the gold standard for investor judgment. But through much of the Enron crisis, as Ken Lay was exuberantly touting the health of Enron stock (while secretly liquidating many of his own Enron holdings), analysts were issuing deceptively optimistic "buy" recommendations.

The analysts' wilding was especially dramatic in the WorldCom debacle. Jack Grubman, one of Wall Street's most respected analysts, issued glowing recommendations about WorldCom stock just days before the telecom giant collapsed. Subsequent e-mail revelations showed an intimate collaboration between Grubman and Bernie Ebbers, the WorldCom founder and chairman, with Grubman coaching Ebbers on business strategy and on how to calm analyst and public concerns about WorldCom as it began to unravel. The touted independence and objectivity of the analyst were obviously fictional, a point made more graphic in another scandal when Grubman acknowledged that he had elevated his rating of AT&T stock because AT&T's boss had helped Grubman's twin daughters get into an exclusive nursery school.[12]

On April 28, 2003, the SEC and state regulators reached a $1.4 billion settlement against 10 of Wall Street's biggest banks for proferring misleading advice to the public. Almost all of the advice involved recommendations to buy when the company was in trouble. One of the most far-reaching and damaging legal settlements ever won by the SEC, it specifically accused Citigroup's Salomon Smith Barney, Merrill Lynch, and Credit Suisse First Boston of fraud, while implicating nearly every other major Wall Street bank in the duping of investors "to curry favor with corporate clients."[13] Analysts' compensation is tied to the amount of banking business they help bring in, partly through buttering up executives by issuing rosy reports on their companies. Ninety-eight percent of analyst recommendations are to buy, reflecting the crony relationships between analysts, the banks that employ them, and the companies they do business with. This problem, finally acknowledged by Wall Street itself, long preceded Enron and is clearly a form of systemic wilding. Analysts were constrained in telling the truth about companies like Enron and WorldCom because the banks that employed the analysts had sunk commercial loans into these companies and were desperate to hold onto the huge lucrative underwriting business that a gloomy analyst report might jeopardize. The analysts' work inevitably became a thinly veiled con job, leading Morgan Stanley analyst Barton Biggs to write that Wall Street "may at times have seemed like a casino, but at least it was an honest casino." Now, as in Las Vegas, small investors wonder whether the house always wins and they are "players in a loser's game."[14]

This systemic wilding emerged from the deregulation of Wall Street and the breakdown of the "Chinese wall" that had historically separated commercial from investing banking as well as banking of both types from research and analyst services. After the 1929 financial crash, where similar crony relations had contributed to loss of faith in the markets, President Franklin Roosevelt passed the Glass-Stegall Act and other regulations preventing commercial banks from engaging in investment banking, brokering sales, or other financial services. In the 1990s bubble, these regulations were systematically dismantled and new financial giants such as Citigroup and Merrill Lynch gobbled up business on both sides of the toppled Chinese wall. Investors are already shunning the advice of the Wall Street analysts, moving to more unbiased sources in independent companies, and many Wall Street firms are eliminating their analyst services or separating their analyst and research divisions completely from other banking services. The only answer to this particular component of systemic wilding on Wall Street: rebuild the wall.

George W. Bush and the Corporate State: Systemic Wilding in Washington, D.C.

After the Enron crisis hit the headlines, George W. Bush proclaimed that corporate criminals would go straight to jail, but then he appointed Harvey Pitt as head of the chief watchdog agency, the Securities and Exchange Commission. Pitt was a lawyer for accounting firms, well known for protecting the rich. The Pitt appointment was just the tip of the iceberg of the political protection system that both Republican and Democratic administrations have lavishly supported. The Bush administration, with a cabinet drawn heavily from the big business community, is the embodiment of the corporate state, which is a melding of corporations and the political class that pursues profit over people. The corporate state helps fuel systemic wilding today, and it continues to grow under both Republican and Democratic presidents.[15]

The close relation between George W. Bush and Kenneth Lay, Enron's CEO, exposed America's corporate state to the glare of public scrutiny.

Bush and Lay were long-time golfing buddies, and Bush scribbled notes addressed to "Kenny boy." Enron was the top contributor to Bush personally over his career, donating $623,000 to him by January 2001. In the 2000 campaign alone, Enron gave $1.5 million to Republican candidates for federal office and the GOP National Committee.[16] Lay was also one of Dick Cheney's energy advisors and was once rumored to be Bush's choice for Secretary of the Treasury. Moreover, many of the Bush administration's top officials had worked for Enron, whose board of directors had long been full of Bush cronies. Wendy Gramm, Secretary of Labor and wife of the powerful former Texas senator Phil Gramm, had served on Enron's audit committee. Secretary of the Army Thomas White, who resigned in 2003, had been Enron's point person in its deceptive and disastrous California operations in electric power trading.

The massive contributions of Enron to Bush paid off richly in Washington. Enron had long sought to dominate a deregulated energy market and Bush was the great champion of energy deregulation. The Bush administration deregulated the energy future contracts market (Enron's most lucrative business) nationally. More broadly, it turned a dull system of regulated markets into a "free for all of energy companies selling electricity back and forth like pork bellies," while resisting efforts by states to regulate Enron business. Enron helped pick Bush's head of the Federal Energy Regulatory Commission that prevented California from imposing essential price controls on this disastrous free-for-all. And to seal the deal, in five secret meetings, Enron executives helped Vice President Dick Cheney craft the Bush administration's overall energy program, which included a major role for Lay in the plan to tap Arctic oil. Cheney invoked executive privilege to resist making the contents of those meetings public.[17]

Nonetheless, there still remained the SEC, the crown jewel of the regulatory system, a commission charged with defending the public from Enron-like abuses. In the five years preceding the collapse, when Enronmania was driving up Enron's stock value by 40 percent each year, the SEC never audited Enron. After the crisis, when it became impossible to ignore the company's wilding, Bush promised to crack down and increase the investigatory powers of the SEC. But when he appointed Pitt as head of the SEC, it became clear that the corporate state was going to protect its own. Pitt's appointment was such a blatant display of corporate influence that it created a huge public outcry, eventually leading to his resignation. The SEC today, however, still lacks the will or resources to prevent future Enrons. The SEC is charged with reviewing the statements of 17,000 public companies and has about 100 lawyers to do it, with the number of senior experts able to decipher the more technical details far smaller. The SEC lacks enough staff even to just read the glossy annual reports of the

17,000 companies, let alone vet the detailed technical statements, supervise the vast mutual funds empire, oversee the financial exchanges, and monitor insider trading. SEC lawyers are paid about one-third less than in other federal agencies and their turnover is over 30 percent—double that of other government agencies. While the SEC launched hundreds of new probes after Enron, most are fading away, dying for lack of will and resources in a Bush regime of, by, and for the corporation.[18]

It would be a mistake, though, to imagine that a Democratic administration would be much different. The corporate state is indifferent to whether the donkey or the elephant is sitting in the White House. Consider that Enron in 2002 had contributed to 71 of the hundred senators as well as to 187 members of the House. The top recipients included Senator Charles Schumer, a Democrat from New York, and Senator Joseph Lieberman of Connecticut, who ran for vice president in 2000 on the Democratic ticket with Al Gore. In the Clinton years, Enron developed close relations with Ron Brown, Clinton's top trade official, who continued Bush Sr.'s practice of helping Enron win lucrative energy contracts in India, the Philippines, Chile, Colombia, and many other countries. All through the Clinton years, Enron was a major political force in Washington, spending money all over K street (the heart of the lobbying industry) and wielding major influence over the White House, Congress, both parties, and major lobbies such as the U.S. Council for International Business and the National Foreign Trade Council.

Enron is just one of hundreds of huge corporations throwing its weight around Washington, far down the list of the biggest political contributors. The Enron case is thus a dramatic but small instance of the larger crisis of the corporate state. The corporate state has become the domineering institution of our times, undermining the prospect of true democracy and running roughshod over the interests of ordinary people. A marriage of corporations and the political class, the corporate state is the engine that drives systemic wilding. It shapes a political and economic system designed to reward the rich at the expense of the general public. The Enron crisis is important mainly because it exposes the wilding dimensions of the corporate state and the larger social system it creates and protects.

The solution to systemic wilding is democracy. Enron was a huge unaccountable corporation, with its top executives wheeling and dealing without having to answer to anyone: its board of directors, federal regulators, its own workers, or the general public. Enron, though, simply symbolizes the lack of accountability built into the larger system in which it is embedded. All the major players—the accountants, regulators, and politicians—work together to insulate their collective wilding from public view or control. How can such a system be made accountable? Only if the public decides that enough is enough and begins to take the constitutional creed of democracy seriously. The corporate state will continue to be an engine of wilding—siphoning power and wealth from ordinary citizens to the rich—until people turn off their corporate-programmed televisions, shrug off their couch-potato identities, and decide to throw the CEOs out of Washington. Then, they will face the task of rebuilding a true democratic system—something that will require imagination, hope, and dedicated activism in a new generation that may be inspired to act by the memory of Enrons past and the frightening prospect of those still to come.

6

Wilding in the Church

Unaccountable Brethren and Voices of the Faithful

While the Enron scandal was sending shock waves throughout America and the world, a new scandal was shaking the nation. Sitting in my office at Boston College, I was seeing it unfold just a few blocks from me. For weeks, I saw television and radio crews, along with police officers, lined up outside the vast seminary buildings and homes where Cardinal Bernard Law—a great prince of the church—lived, just down Commonwealth Avenue from BC. The reporters were waiting for the cardinal to come out and give them an account of what he had known about priest sexual abuse and when he knew it. The police were there to keep order as angry groups of laity congregated to demand Law's resignation. And every morning, when I sat down to breakfast and opened my *New York Times* and *Boston Globe*, I read another headline about the sickening litany of abuse cases and the alleged cover-up by Law and the other esteemed leaders of the church.

As I read the papers, I often saw one story about Enron and another about the church on the same page. A reader (especially a sociologist) could hardly avoid seeing some parallels. Here were two of the world's great institutions—the corporation and the church—imploding in sensational scandals. In both cases, the leaders at the top faced charges of gross ethical and criminal misconduct. They had protected themselves at the expense of those who had put their trust in them, and they had been getting away with it for years. When the truth began to spill out, they launched massive coverups. In both cases, leaders had hijacked their institutions from the "laity" and had faced no accountability. Both cases were institutional wilding on a grand, systemic scale.

Wilding in the church is in many respects more shocking than in the business world. We expect greed and deception in the business world. But the business of the church is morality, and we expect the church to model the highest standards of conduct. Societies look to their great religious institutions to teach and inspire moral commitments, and when they fail to do so, societies themselves are at risk of unraveling. This has been part of the central teaching of social theorists who created the modern discipline of sociology. The great French sociologist, Émile Durkheim, argued that collective moral codes are the glue of societies throughout history. The agents of these moral codes may change over time, and Durkheim thought the professions and a new division of labor in the economy might supplant traditional religious institutions as the most important sources of solidarity and moral cohesion. But sociologists since Durkheim have seen religious institutions as integral to the survival of morality and society itself.

Wilding in the church is, then, arguably the most dangerous type. If it signals a broad decline in the integrity of religious institutions, it could turn wilding into a social epidemic, triggering the type of complete breakdown of moral restraint found among the Ik. The wilding in the Catholic Church is frightening because it appears to mirror wilding in the corporate world, in the government, and in other core American institutions, suggesting systemic wilding on a very broad level. And it has the potential to destroy the faith of Americans in anything but looking out for number one.

I need to caution here that my observations in this chapter are about the church as a social, political, and administrative institution, not about Catholicism as a faith or doctrine. Teaching at a Catholic institution has reinforced my sense of the power of the Catholic faith to inspire courage and commitment to social justice. I see this demonstrated by my students, mostly Catholic, who impress me every day with their humanity and dedication to making the world more compassionate and just. My wilding story here is not a reflection on Catholic faith but a commentary on how the power hierarchies that corrupt so many of our institutions have corrupted the institutional church. And as at Enron, the solution involves creating institutional accountability by empowering the laity, something that I show is entirely consistent with the canononical law of the church.

Pedophilia, Sexual Abuse, and Rape: Wilding among the Priests

In 2002, the *Boston Globe* Spotlight Team, a group of crack investigative journalists, broke the story. In a series of devastating reports, they showed that hundreds of priests in the Boston archdiocese had been committing

78

repeated acts of sexual abuse against young boys and girls entrusted to them. One of the early priest offenders was John J. Geoghan, a now-convicted child molester. Eighty-six people have filed civil lawsuits against Geoghan and his superiors, arguing that he had assaulted them over a period of almost 35 years, and more than 130 people have testified since the mid-1990s that Geoghan molested or raped them as he was moved around six Boston parishes over three decades. Almost all were young boys in elementary schools when Geoghan assaulted them, one as young as 4 years old.[1]

In the 1980s, Geoghan targeted his victims by honing in on young Catholic mothers, often single parents, working overtime to hold their large families together. Geoghan would offer to help by taking the kids for ice cream or helping them pray in their bedrooms. The *Globe* reported that one of the victims, 12-year-old Patrick McSorley, was lured by ice cream. In the car after buying ice cream for Patrick, Geoghan "patted his upper leg and slid his hand up toward his crotch." McSorley said, "I froze. I didn't know what to think. Then he put his hand on my genitals and started masturbating me. I was petrified." Geoghan then began masturbating himself. When he let Patrick out of the car, he said this was a secret between the two of them and that "we're very good at keeping secrets."[2]

Another horrific story involves the priest Paul Shanley, who was transferred to a parish in California after reported abuses in the Boston archdiocese. Church records show allegations of Shanley's abuse of children dating back to the 1960s. In May 2003 Shanley was indicted for raping a six-year-old multiple times. Shanley has been accused of raping at least 26 children, including Gregory Ford, now 24, who alleges he was raped from the time he was 6 to 11. Ford's attorney, Roderick MacLeish, said, "This man was a monster in the archdiocese of Boston for many, many years." Ford called Shanley's long service to the church a "reign of terror."[3]

A remarkable feature of the Shanley story is that Shanley had openly advocated sex between men and boys for years. In the 1970s, he had explicitly embraced this position in an address to the North American Man-Boy Love Association. Moreover, after the Boston archdiocese transferred him to St. Anne's parish in San Bernardino, California, Shanley and another priest, John J. White, opened up a bed-and-breakfast inn for gay customers while still on the payroll of the church. Shanley, a former street priest, and White operated a substantial business, including multiple motel cabins on two plots of property in Palm Springs called Whispering Palms and the Cabana Club resort.[4]

More than 1,200 priests have now been accused of criminal sexual or other abuse. These include a priest accused of beating and terrorizing a housekeeper, one who traded cocaine for sex, and one who enticed teenage girls into having sex, comparing himself to Jesus Christ. At this writing, a growing scandal about rape of girls as well as boys is threatening to add more fuel to this never-ending story.[5]

Cardinal Bernard Law and the Cover-up: The Church as Institutional Wilder

The sexual exploitation of young children is a horrific form of expressive wilding by individuals, made worse when carried out by priests entrusted with tending to their spiritual needs. The numbers of priests and victims is overwhelming, and were this the whole story it would be tragedy enough. But the more important dimension of the story for our purposes is not the individual wilding by priests but the institutional wilding carried out by the top clerical hierarchy. The conduct of the clerical princes reveals that the church itself, viewed not theologically as a faith but sociologically as a complex organization, is an engine of institutional wilding, a matter of the gravest concern in what many view as the most important moral institution on the planet.

Cardinal Law, one of the most powerful and esteemed American clerics before the crisis, with close ties to the Vatican, tragically illustrates the transformation of the institutional church into a wilding system. On September 18, 2002, 27 people who claimed to be sexual assault victims filed a civil lawsuit accusing Cardinal Law, other top bishops, and the archdiocese itself with covering up sexual abuse by priests for 50 years. Three months later the cardinal, who had denied the charges almost to the end, resigned, unable to sustain financial contributions to the diocese or to maintain his moral authority in light of the facts coming to the courts. Outrage about Law's conduct spread from the victims to leading Catholics in the business community, universities, the media, and the political establishment.

Ultimately, Law was forced to admit in court that he had known of many of the priests who repeatedly raped and abused young children—and that he had not reported the facts to the courts nor prevented the repeat-abusers from continuing to do pastoral work among young people. Law defended his behavior by saying that in some of the cases priests had received counseling and that in others there was insufficient evidence to make a conclusive opinion about guilt. He also expressed belief in the redemptive power of faith and healing for priests, and the responsibility of the church to help them.

Law's pattern of behavior was to protect the abuser-priest rather than the victim, typically by shuttling him to a new parish. Geoghan was a glaring example, with Law transferring him from St. Paul's parish in Hingham in 1974, from St. Andrew's in Jamaica Plain in 1980, and from St. Brendan's in Dorechester in 1984. In each case, there were voluminous records in the archdiocese showing molestation, as well as rumors widely spread among priests and housekeepers about Geoghan bringing altar boys into his rectory rooms and having them in the showers.[6]

Law not only repeatedly reassigned Geoghan to new parishes, but added grave insult to injury by having his aides tell traumatized victims to remain silent. Bishop Thomas Daily, a top Law aide, acknowledged that he "may well have" encouraged seven abuse victims of Geoghan who lived in Jamaica Plain to "keep quiet." They had a responsibility to do this, he said, to protect the church from scandal.[7]

Protection for priests who abuse was also proffered to Paul Shanley. As the Boston archdiocese had received allegations and reports about Shanley's sexual abuses and open advocacy of sex between men and boys, it continued to reassign him to new parishes. In 1990 Law's top aide, Bishop Robert Banks, wrote a letter to a San Bernardino, California, diocese vouching for Shanley's good record and integrity, despite internal reports in the Boston archdiocese that he had allegedly molested three boys. An attorney for a victim claimed that the archdiocese was doing anything possible to keep Shanley out of Boston, hoping to spare Cardinal Law the embarrassment and potential liability of Shanley's presence.[8]

Geoghan and Shanley were only the tip of the iceberg. Cardinal Law kept the Reverend James D. Foley on active parish service after he knew that a woman died of a drug overdose following an evening of sex with the priest. After a conversation with Reverend Jay Mullin, who had been accused of several molestations and removed from several parishes, Law reinstated Mullin in 1998 as parish vicar without telling the new congregation that the church had paid a secret settlement of $60,000 to settle an earlier case against Mullin. While the cardinal continued to deny knowing about or reassigning abusive priests, church records turned over to a Boston court after a civil suit filed by victims in 2002 showed otherwise. Judge Constance M. Sweeney wrote that over 11,000 documents showed clear evidence of reassigning priests who were abusers. Meanwhile, records showed that the church had paid thousands upon thousands of dollars to victims in secret settlements over the past two decades to buy their silence.

The archdiocese went to great lengths to keep its records out of view of the courts and the public, claiming legal immunity for charitable institutions and arguing that the constitutional separation of church and state created the right of the church to keep its records secret. Judge Sweeney, calling this "an increasingly dreary effort" by church lawyers to hide documents. On July 24, 2003, after a 16-month investigation, Massachusetts Attorney General Thomas F. Reilly concluded that Cardinal Law and his subordinate bishops facilitated abuse and protected abuser-priests for years. "The mistreatment of children was so massive and so prolonged that it borders on the unbelievable," Reilly said. The church leaders, he said, "in effect, sacrificed children for many, many years."

Cardinal Law's protection of priests over victims is unfortunately not a unique practice, but a pattern increasingly being revealed in dioceses all over the country. Some are run by protégés of Law in Wisconsin, New Hampshire, and New York, but victims have alleged similar cover-ups in archdioceses from California to Florida. As the crisis became national, the U.S. Conference of Catholic Bishops convened to develop a new policy, and the Vatican itself began to get involved. The bishops promised a new policy of zero tolerance, but the laity and public have yet to be convinced, not unreasonably since Cardinal Law had pronounced such a policy in 1994.

Enron, the Corporate State, and the Church: Wilding and the Collapse of Institutional Accountability

In the previous chapter, I showed that Enron's wilding grew out of a hijacking of the corporation by its chief executives, who ran it without accountability to their workers or the public. There is a striking parallel with the Boston archdiocese and the institutional church more broadly. Top church administrators run their organizational empires with virtually no accountability to their laity. Sociologically, the wilding that follows is an entirely predictable outcome of vesting exclusive power in the princely brethren.

Enron became a major crisis because the one group to which the executive brethren were legally accountable—the shareholders—were key victims of the scandal. The Enron crisis showed that the accountability to even this legally enfranchised group had collapsed. This created a crisis of legitimacy about capitalism among investors whose faith is essential to the operation of the system.

The church crisis has an eerie parallel. The mission of the church is to serve the spiritual needs of the laity, a group similar to the shareholders and workers in the Enron crisis. As I detail shortly, there are elements of canon law which specify that the clerical brethren are, in fact, accountable to the laity organizationally as well as spiritually. But the current crisis shows that, as with Enron, the brethren have captured the institution for themselves and are prepared to protect their own at whatever cost to the laity they are supposed to serve.

Priests have made this argument forcefully. The Reverend James J. Scahill, a pastor at St. Michael's parish in Springfield, Massachusetts, wrote a public letter to his bishop, Thomas L. Dupre, scolding him for dragging his feet on removing a priest convicted of abusing boys. The bishop accused him of disobedience, but Scahill believes that the hierarchy of the church wanted a dangerous type of authority. "The kind of obedience he's looking for," Scahill says, "is the obedience of the soldiers of Hitler—a blind, myopic obedience."[10] Scahill charges that the top bishops are seeking, for their own ends, to keep the institutional church immune from scrutiny by the laity, the public, and the courts. "The bishops are spending more time with their lawyers than with their consciences."[11] Regarding the brethren's efforts to protect themselves by invoking the constitutional separation of church and state, he says, "I don't hold the institutional church to be superior to justice. It's made me ashamed to be a Catholic."[12]

Scahill offers a keen observation about the core of the problem: the hierarchy's disposition to "protect the institution at all costs." The historical example he uses is startling. "In some real way, we're the last of the landed gentry. They give us beautiful houses to live in, housekeepers to clean. Who else has that? . . . I think priests have become content with their little fiefdoms . . . and I think that's the reason for the silence."[13]

This hints at the parallel between the Enron crisis and the church's. In both cases, the princely "brethren"—whether CEOs or archbishops—have hijacked an institution, eliminated any countervailing power, created a culture of secrecy or nontransparency, and used their unaccountable authority to serve their own interests. To protect their privileged lifestyle, they have been willing to sacrifice their respective laity, whether shareholders or parishioners, and render them mute. Without a voice, the laity has become vulnerable to horrible abuse that can only be described as institutionalized systemic wilding.

The similarity between corporate and church wilding is not sociologically surprising. The church is one of the world's great corporate empires, historically one of the wealthiest institutions, possessed of vast land, great buildings, and thousands of employees. The material wealth of the institutional church remains formidably large, and the princes of the church enjoy enormous privileges of lifestyle, status, and political power. They consort closely with business and political elites in the corporate state, a part of the broader social elite in America. They have embraced the organizational structure of the other great hierarchal institutions, including the corporation and the military. And as in these other institutions, they have succumbed to the inevitable temptations to monopolize power and information to help themselves and protect their own. As they disenfranchise the laity, it is sociologically entirely predictable that the lack of accountability leads to wilding. Tragically, self-interest and exploitation are becoming as integral to the structure of the institutional church as they are to the corporation and the corporate state.

How to End Wilding in the Church: Empower the Laity

Reverend Scahill concludes that "there needs to be other voices out there. A healthy church requires change."[14] The institutional church is not exempt from the structural imperatives essential to any vast complex organization. To heal itself from the wilding curse, it needs the same remedy as Enron and the corporate state in Washington, D.C. It must reconnect with the laity and empower them with knowledge, voice, and governance authority. The unaccountable institutional system is predisposed to become a cesspool of uncontrollable wilding.

In the corporate world, preventing institutional wilding means putting worker and public representatives on the board of directors, flattening the corporate hierarchy, institutionalizing transparency, and creating an entirely new system of public regulation and accountability. This, of course, means nothing short of democratizing the corporation and its captive government in Washington. Both the corporation and the government must become institutions of, by, and for the people.

But is such a democratic system of accountability possible or even desirable in the institutional church? Many might conclude that both history and doctrine make the institutional church unique, one that must inevitably be a hierarchy ruled by the princes at the top. Others disagree, and some of the most interesting voices are those of the faithful that are emerging in the wake of the current crisis.

In Boston, the epicenter of the crisis, a bold group of laity formed to demand that the church listen and change to ensure that sexual abuse never again occur in the church. Calling themselves the Voice of the Faithful, they have become a global organization of more than 30,000 practicing Catholics.[15] They see themselves as "mainstream" Catholics, but they conclude that the institutional church needs to end its culture of secrecy and empower the laity to prevent future scandals. They see this as entirely consistent with their faith and with the vision of the institutional church expressed in the Second Vatican Council, a historic papal initiative between 1962 and 1965 that called for more social justice and democratic church reforms.

A fundamental principle of Voice of the Faithful is that "the Church should respect the dignity and intelligence of the laity . . . and work for active and meaningful engagement of the laity in the operations of the Church. . . . " Drawing on Vatican II, the organization proposes "to empower an active Parish Pastoral Council in every parish." They also propose creating "parallel Lay councils on intermediate levels such as the vicariate and the region. . . . " Voice of the Faithful sees participation by the laity in church governance as central to preventing future abuse and regards the church's current culture of "secrecy and exclusion" as incompatible with the church's health.[16]

Organizations seeking to bring more openness, democracy, and accountability to the church existed long before the current crisis. The Association for the Rights of Catholics in the Church (ARCC) is a federation of the laity in many European countries, including France, Germany, Great Britain, Ireland, Italy, Belgium, and others. ARCC is affiliated with the European Conference for Human Rights in the Church and is also inspired by the vision of the Second Vatican Council. It is part of a worldwide movement to promote social justice and democracy in and outside of the church.[17]

ARCC believes that "the message of the Gospel mandates a concern for justice in the Church, as well as in the world." Thus the rights of Catholics must be respected and embodied in the structure of the institutional church as well as in the broader society. It believes the rights of Catholics in the church "derive both from our basic humanity as persons and from our baptism as Christians."[18]

ARCC's Charter of Rights includes sections on basic rights, decision-making and dissent, due process, and social and cultural rights, as well as ministries and spirituality. It reads remarkably like the 1948 U.N. Declaration of Universal Human Rights and is essentially a manifesto for democratizing the institutional church. Regarding decision-making, it proposes that "all Catholics have the right to a voice in all decisions that affect them, including the choosing of their leaders." Should there be any doubt that this is a call for democratic accountability, the Charter's sixth provision is that "all Catholics have the right to have their leaders accountable to them."[19]

The fascinating feature of ARCC is that it explicitly roots these Catholic rights in the church within canon law, the body of official codes that governs the institutional church, although it views canon law as only a "partial" statement of the necessary just relation between the church and its faithful. The right to participate in all decisions is rooted in Canon 212.3 of the 1983 revised Canon Law code, which mandates that the faithful "have the right, and even at times a duty" to express their views. The right to accountability is drawn from Canon 492, which mandates in each diocese a finance council "composed of at least three members of the laity," and from Canon 1287.2, which states that "administrators are to render an account to the faithful. . . . " AARC references many other canon laws that spell out the rights of the laity to form associations and express their views freely on all matters within the church.[20]

ARCC, drawing on the social justice teachings set forth in Pope Paul VI's "Populorum Progressio," says that justice requires "the renewal of the Church's own structural organization. . . . " Underlying the entire Charter of Catholic Rights is the principle that "all Catholics are radically equal." This is rooted in Canon 208, which states: "There exists among all the Christian faithful, in virtue of their rebirth in Christ, a true equality with regard to dignity and activity. . . . "

While one of his great concerns was the separation between church and state, Thomas Jefferson articulated the same philosophy of radical equality in the Declaration of Independence, and there is a similar vision of human rights in the Bill of Rights to the Constitution. The United Nation's Declaration of Rights is more expansive than Jefferson's in its vision of social and economic rights and more parallel to the philosophy of comprehensive rights now being articulated by the church's rising "voices of the faithful." While they should be kept separate, the institutional church and the corporate state must be renewed with a similar vision of rights and democratic accountability if they are to prevent the princely brethren, corporate and clerical, from dominating both spheres and plunging us further into a systemic wilding epidemic. Fortunately, new grassroots movements are rising to challenge the princes in all the great hierarchies of society and offer hope of a more democratized and moral order.

who they might be, when my thoughts are interrupted and they start talking to me.

I'm a bit nervous, but I don't show any emotion. They ask for my name and where I'm from, which I ignore and keep looking straight ahead. They don't give up. I am sitting no more than a foot away from them. The only thing that separates us is skinny bars making up a cage around my seat. What if they spit at me, or worse? Somebody gets up from their seat and starts singing what sounds like a love song in Spanish, and I begin to relax a little. It seems like almost all of them are speaking Spanish. Unexpectedly, the guy who is singing switches from Spanish to flawless English and speaks directly to me. He's saying he saw a brochure that says inmates can get married in jail. He says he's twenty-five, doesn't have kids, and that we should get married. The other men start laughing and somebody's telling him that he's probably not my type. Then a few others try to talk to me all at the same time. I hear different kinds of questions coming from different directions. I keep looking straight ahead and ignore them all. Then they collectively try to guess where I'm from. They compliment my glasses and clothes. They tell me jokes and try to make me smile.

<hr>

It feels like at least half an hour has passed, and most of the men have given up trying to talk to me. Somebody says I would do well in an interrogation. Then some guy gives a little speech, saying that he doesn't know whether I understand Spanish or not, but he wishes me luck and says that everything will be okay. That's what I have been telling myself the past few hours, that everything will be okay. I'm surprised by their compassion. At this point I'm fighting back my tears. I look down at my leggings and I see a little red thread from my daughter's blanket. Just a few hours ago, I was holding her in my arms wrapped in a red blanket.

<hr>

Somebody says we're almost there, which initiates the men talking to me again. They tell me I'll be okay, that they hope to see me in court, and that they wish me luck with my case. The driver opens my

Killing Society

The Ungluing of America

A nation never falls but by suicide.

—Ralph Waldo Emerson

An American Dream that does not spell out the moral consequences of unmitigated self-interest threatens to turn the next generation of Americans into wilding machines. In a pattern already visible today, Americans could turn not only on each other but on society as well, too self-absorbed to make the commitments and observe the moral constraints that hold stable communities together. There is already abundant evidence that a wilder generation of Americans is assaulting and abandoning society, allowing the guarantees of civilized behavior and the most vital social institutions to languish and die as this generation pursues its own selfish dreams.

The breakdown of society that I describe in this chapter—from violence on the streets to state violence, from broken schools to broken politics—is a cause as well as a consequence of the wilding crisis. The wilding culture poisons families, workplaces, and neighborhoods, which in their weakened form are fertile spawning grounds for more wilding. There is no first cause in this chicken-and-egg causal chain; the wilding virus creates social breakdown and simultaneously grows out of it.

Wilding in the Streets

America's culture of wilding, at its extreme, is triggering an epidemic of bizarre and terrifying violence. The new violence constitutes a direct assault on society, threatening the social infrastructure that sustains civilized life.

On February 1, 2001, police arrested a 9-year-old boy who allegedly attacked four of his schoolmates with a hypodermic needle. Running through the gymnasium in Public School 66 in Brooklyn, New York, he reportedly stabbed two boys and two girls, who had to be rushed to the hospital.[1] A yet more bizarre needle attack took place on New York City streets some years earlier, when 10 teenage girls were arrested and "charged with jabbing women with pins in dozens of unprovoked attacks on the Upper West Side over a one-week period." The girls "thought it was fun to run down Broadway," Deputy Police Chief Ronald Fenrich said, and stick "women with pins to see their reactions." The girls expressed some remorse, Fenrich reported, although mainly "they were sorry they got caught." Meanwhile, the neighborhood residents, although they had seen more vicious crimes, told reporters that they found the pinprick attacks an "intolerable invasion, both because of the cavalier manner in which the attacks were carried out, and because rumors spread early that it was possible the jabs had come from AIDS-infected needles."[2]

American cities have always been violent places, but the pinprick attacks are emblematic of a new, more menacing violence and a more profound breakdown of social life. Like the expressive wilding in Central Park, the attacks involve taking pleasure in the inflicting of pain and complete indifference to the sensibilities of the victims. The potential targets—anyone walking the street—need to become hypervigilant and assume that every pedestrian is a potential threat.

The horrifying image of children killing children has helped define our era. In February 2001, a Florida jury convicted Lionel Tate, 12, of first-degree murder for killing a 6-year-old girl while practicing wrestling moves he had seen on television. Just two weeks later, Massachusetts police arrested an 11-year-old boy for stabbing another boy to death in a Springfield movie theater. Less than two years earlier, a 10-year-old Massachusetts boy was charged with murdering a 5-week-old baby.

The epidemic of kids murdering kids first grabbed public attention in the 1990s. In October 1994 two Chicago boys, aged 10 and 11, threw 5-year-old Erik Morris to his death from a fourteenth-floor window. The reason: Erik had refused to steal candy for them. Erik's 8-year-old brother had desperately tried to save him but was overpowered by the bigger boys.

A month earlier, Chicagoan Robert Sandifer, aged 11, was killed by two boys, aged 14 and 16, who feared that Sandifer would squeal about their gang activities to police. Shortly before his own murder, Sandifer had killed a 14-year-old girl, Shavan Dean, when he fired a volley of bullets into a group of teenagers playing football. Young Sandifer was buried with his teddy bear.

Violent crime throughout the United States peaked in the mid-1990s, but rates of murder, armed burglary, and other violent crimes remain exceptionally high—far higher than in Western European nations, Japan, and other developed countries. A November 2000 survey of 10 thousand youths aged 12 to 17 documents that violence is rampant. Funded by 18 federal agencies, the study reports that one out of four students, representing about 5.3 million American children, "told investigators they had either used a gun or knife, carried such a weapon or had been involved in an incident in which someone was injured by a weapon in the past year." Robert Blum, the principal researcher, concluded that "the prevalence of violence is much higher than we expected, particularly when you consider we've taken out all the fistfighting that seventh- and eighth-grade boys do." He might have added that the study also factored out the violence rates among the astonishing number of young people whom we have locked up in federal and state prisons.[3]

School violence is now widely considered a national crisis in itself. On February 29, 2000, a 6-year-old child allegedly fired a .32-caliber pistol at a 6-year-old girl in a classroom at Buell Elementary School near Flint, Michigan. According to eyewitnesses, the boy tucked the gun in his pants, pulled it out, and fired, striking her in the neck. He then reportedly ran into a nearby bathroom and threw the gun into a trash can. The girl, Kayla Rolland, died 30 minutes later. According to one report, the motive might have arisen out of a scuffle between the two on the playground the day before.[4]

The U.S. Center for Disease Control reports that almost 10 percent of children bring a weapon to school. School violence peaked in the early 1990s, but incidents with multiple fatalities have increased, the most famous being the 1999 massacre at Columbine High School in Littleton, Colorado. At Columbine, two students in black trench coats opened fire with semiautomatic machine guns and killed 15 people and wounded more than 20 others. As in many of these incidents, the motives for this expressive wilding involved jealousy and revenge for being excluded from the most popular circles—the rage of the outcast. But they also mirrored the violent culture of the school that they hated. Columbine put the toughest football players on a pedestal, honoring physical force. The Columbine area also has a strong military presence, and the young killers had grown up infatuated with war and surrounded by guns.

The chronicle of school violence in the last decade is stupefying. On December 6, 1999, a 13-year-old student in Fort Gibson, Oklahoma, came to school and shot at least four of his classmates with his father's nine-millimeter semiautomatic weapon. A few weeks earlier, a 12-year-old boy in a Deming, New Mexico, middle school shot and killed a female classmate, aged 12, in the schoolyard. On May 15, 1998, a 15-year-old student in Springfield, Ohio, killed two classmates in the school cafeteria. On May 21, 1998, police reported that three sixth-grade boys had a "hit list" and had been plotting to kill many of their classmates in a sniper attack at school during a false fire alarm. A few months earlier, in a high school in West Paducah, Kentucky, a 14-year-old student killed three students and wounded five others while they were participating in a prayer circle in a school hallway. And a few months before that, a 16-year-old student in Pearl, Mississippi, shot and killed his mother and then shot nine students at school.[5]

Children themselves are terrified in many schools and neighborhoods. Fourteen-year-old Chirll Rivers is a Boston student who says she's scared: "I don't want to die. You have to watch your back every day. Someone could mistake you for someone else and shoot you. I could be the wrong person."[6] Another kid, forced to walk home from a youth program after a van broke down, collapsed in a panic, crying, "I can't walk home, I just can't walk home. Someone got killed on my street. I'll get killed too." The *Boston Globe* reported that this youth did get home, running all the way, but that in the next eight days, three young men did not have the same luck—killed on the same street—while a fourth was fatally shot through the window of his mother's apartment. The result of this unprecedented epidemic of violence, the *Globe* said, was that "increasing numbers of city youths are arming themselves, carrying small knives and pistols tucked into their waistbands or inside their coats."[7]

A new wave of school violence erupted in Boston schools in 2001, creating a crisis in the city. On January 19, 2001, a parent attacked a first-grade teacher, who was sent to the hospital with a black eye and fractured cheekbone. Within three weeks of this incident, an eighth-grader punched an assistant principal and a knife-wielding ninth-grader chased a track coach. A week later, assailants with knives stabbed boys in two different schools. According to the National Center for Education Statistics, despite a reduction in juvenile crime rates, the national percentage of students saying they felt too unsafe to go to school at least once per month grew to 5.2 percent in 1999, compared to 4 percent in 1997. And, according to another study released in 2001, a majority of U.S. teenagers used violence in the last year, and one in five boys brought a weapon to high school. "The seeds of violence," said Institute of Ethics President Michael Josephson, who funded the study, "can be found in schools all over America."[8]

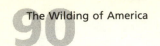

Falling Bridges, Potholes, and Peeling Schoolroom Paint: The Abandonment of Society

Journalist Tom Ashbrook, returning from a long trip to Asia, records his initial impressions of Los Angeles. "Hello Occident. Cracked highways, no service. Hotel is heavy on glitter and self-promotional hype, light on everything else. Construction quality shabby. Rusting metalwork. Cheap materials. . . . Rich next to poor. Slick by shabby. Twitchy bag ladies and a legless panhandler croaking 'Aloha.' . . . Korean cabdriver complains road repairs take ten times longer than in Seoul."[9]

"An American homecoming," Ashbrook groans, "is a journey into shades of disarray." It is downright "scary for a recent returnee." Ashbrook, who is returning from a 10-year sojourn in Asia, learns that his brother-in-law "sleeps with a large pistol in his nightstand and an alarm system that can track a burglar room by room." Turning on the radio, Ashbrook hears of "Los Angeles drivers taking potshots at one another on the freeway, American schoolchildren scoring at the bottom of the first-world heap in key subjects. Drug lords reigning over urban fiefs, Alcoholics Anonymous and its ilk as a new religion. Wall Street sapping the economy." Fresh into his hotel, Ashbrook's son flicks on a Saturday morning cartoon: "Hey, fella! This is America," booms the wisecracking voice of an animated hero. "I've got the right to not work any time I want."[10]

"Our cracked highways and rusting bridges," writes Ashbrook, "seem physical reflections of falling standards, organization, simple care in the performance of jobs—of lost resolve." Ashbrook concludes that a "returning American comes home with trepidation," hoping that his or her sense of the breakdown of America "is exaggerated, fearing that it might not be, subtly prepared to accept it as fact."[11]

Ashbrook is seeing the unmistakable signs of a looming breakdown in both the physical and social infrastructure necessary to keep a society viable. America's physical infrastructure—its grid of roads, bridges, railways, ports, airports, sewer systems, and communications nodes—is in serious disrepair. This is no surprise to the folks in Covington, Tennessee, where a bridge over the Hatchie River collapsed, sending 7 motorists to their deaths; nor to people in upstate New York, where the collapse of a bridge killed 10 people. Nearly half of the 29,000 bridges in Massachusetts are officially "substandard." Two-thirds of these are so badly broken-down that they need to be replaced. Moreover, 70 percent of

Massachusetts roads are rated "fair" or "poor." Almost everywhere "the nation's roads are crumbling . . . existing highways go unrepaired while new ones seldom advance beyond the blueprint stage. Forty percent of the nation's bridges have serious deficiencies. Highways are strained beyond capacity, while potential mass transit options go unexplored. Water delivery systems are so antiquated that some cities still transport water through nineteenth-century wooden pipes." California Democratic congressman Robert T. Matsui says, "The problem is absolutely catastrophic." Rebuilding the national infrastructure, Massachusetts transportation secretary Frederick P. Salvucci says, "is the greatest public works challenge since the pyramids were built."[12]

As the physical infrastructure erodes, the social infrastructure is being quietly starved, creating an emergency in the provision of affordable housing, jobs at a livable wage, basic health care, education, and the social services required to sustain the social fabric. The crisis of affordable housing has now yielded "over three million homeless people," writes journalist Michael Albert, "who wander our backstreets eating out of garbage cans and sleeping under tattered newspapers in bedrooms shared with alley-rats." About 13 percent of Americans have fallen through the slashed social safety net and are poor, partly reflecting the unpleasant reality of an economy churning out a high proportion of extremely low wage jobs. More than 45 million Americans have no health insurance. This includes one-fifth of all American children, contributing to America's life expectancy being lower and the infant mortality rate higher than in all Western European countries and some Eastern European ones as well. Meanwhile, the collapse of American public education is yielding an average American high school student who not only has difficulty locating France, Israel, or the United States itself on a map, but scores lower across the board than students in virtually all the other advanced industrialized countries. This is well understood by American parents, who shun the public school system when they can afford to do so. An estimated 9 out of 10 Boston parents send their children to parochial school or any place other than a Boston public school.[13]

Parents recognize that American public schools are literally disintegrating. A 1995 report by the General Accounting Office showed that 25 thousand U.S. schools housing 14 million children need extensive physical rehabilitation, including New York City schools with exposed asbestos, rotting roof beams, and broken plumbing; Montana schools where water leaks have led to collapsed ceilings; and a New Orleans school where termites have eaten books on library shelves and then the shelves themselves.[14]

This abject unraveling of the social fabric is the ultimate manifestation of the new wilding culture, an abandonment of society consciously engineered by the country's political leadership and passively endorsed by the majority of voters. The cost of maintaining and reconstructing its physical and social infrastructure is well within the reach of the world's still-richest country; however, in what may be the greatest act of domestic-policy wilding, recent presidents, while continuing to pour billions into the Pentagon's coffers, have refused to support the public spending that would halt and reverse the crumbling infrastructure. This refusal is rationalized under the umbrella of "free-market" ideology, to wit: rolling back taxes, deficits, and "big government." In contrast, Western European countries such as Belgium, France, West Germany, and the Netherlands, all less wealthy than the United States, have managed to preserve much of their social infrastructure by spending a substantially higher percentage of their gross national product on health care, education, and a wide range of other social programs.[15]

The End of Government? Compassionate Conservatives, New Democrats, and Political Wilding

George W. Bush campaigned as a "compassionate conservative" who would "leave no child behind." While the rhetoric is appealing, the reality behind the words is less palatable. About one in every five children in America is poor, and it will take billions in education and social services to help get them out of poverty. But by making huge trillion-dollar tax cuts the center of his presidency, Bush has undercut the children. His tax cuts will require taking money from the poor and middle class and recycling it to the rich. Moreover, as the president himself acknowledged, social spending by most federal departments will have to be slashed to make the tax cuts possible, meaning that social programs for the needy will be sliced to return huge sums to the wealthy.

Massive tax-cutting has become a prime and enduring symbol of the new public-policy wilding. Cynically fueled by politicians from both parties (Democrats in 2001 advocated a "modest" tax cut of almost $1 trillion), the so-called tax revolt has created the political space that leaders need to defund society and reflects the war in Americans' hearts and minds between their commitments to society and to themselves. Cutting taxes has become the respectable political vehicle for lashing out at the poor and

ultimately abandoning both government and society itself. Future historians may come to view American leaders playing the tax revolt as a sequel to Nero playing his fiddle as Rome burned.

As described shortly, tax cuts are the centerpiece of George W. Bush's presidency, with Bush seeking to complete the revolution inaugurated by Ronald Reagan. Tax cuts were at the heart of the 1980s Reagan revolution, and Reagan defined himself as a warrior against "big government." Newt Gingrich and his Republican colleagues who took over Congress in 1995, following in Reagan's footsteps, put tax-cutting at the center of their Contract with America and proposed drastically cutting nearly all social spending, from education to health care to welfare.

The Contract's tax and spending cuts were part of a systematic plan to dismantle much of the federal government itself, that is, nearly everything but military and police functions and the corporate welfare policies that provide subsidies for the rich and sustain corporate profitability. Gingrich described this as part of the historic Third Wave revolution conceived by futurists Alvin and Heidi Toffler, which would sweep away central government and "devolve" power and resources to state or local governments. Despite the faddishness of the Tofflerian perspective and the dangers of "states' rights movements," which have historically helped preserve segregation and intolerance, Gingrich translated Third Wave "devolution" into a recipe for "zeroing out" a remarkable array of the most socially protective parts of the government. Among the hundreds of agencies targeted for extinction or zero public funding were the Department of Education, the National Public Broadcasting Service, the Department of Housing and Urban Development, the National Endowment for the Humanities, the National Endowment for the Arts, much of the Environmental Protection Agency, and the Federal Drug Administration.

Although in his 1995 State of the Union address President Clinton repeated his rhetorical commitment to a "new covenant" for social reconstruction, in practice he rushed to join the Tofflerian and tax revolutions, entering into competition with Republicans to see who could cut taxes and government faster. Not only did he propose his own multibillion-dollar tax cuts, targeted largely to the educated middle class rather than the rich or poor, but he also sponsored, in the name of "reinventing government," an unprecedented Democratic war on government itself. Among the agencies that the Clinton administration proposed to eliminate, privatize, or radically shrink were the Federal Aviation Administration, the Department of Transportation, the Interstate Commerce Commission, the Department of Energy, the Department of Housing, the General Services Administration, and the Office of Personnel Management. One hundred and thirty programs, including many for education, scientific research, environmental protection, and welfare, would be terminated. As one Washington observer noted: "You expect to see Republicans, when they are in power, do this—it's what they've been pushing for years. But to see Democrats doing it, and to see the competition between the White House and the Congress as they race to privatize—it's amazing."[16]

Clinton declared his own presidency the "end of big government." He showed he was serious by "ending welfare as we know it." The end of the welfare system, while celebrated in an era of hostility to government and the poor, has thrown millions of people into poverty. Although many former welfare recipients found jobs, most of the jobs do not pay enough to live on. If Clinton had replaced welfare with new programs to support working mothers with child care, affordable housing, health insurance, and a living wage, his policy might have succeeded. But by signing on to the war on government, he was not able to get Congress to fund new social safety nets.

George W. Bush has picked up where his predecessors left off, disguising his political wilding under the rubric of compassion. He acknowledges, indeed boasts, that his trillion-dollar tax cuts are the core domestic mission of his presidency and an attack on the welfare state. But he argues that by downsizing government, through the vehicle of tax-cutting, all will benefit, including the poor. His income tax program, indeed, cuts everyone's taxes, and Bush insists this will give all Americans more control over money that is deservedly their own.

The problem is that most of the billions being returned to the people will go to the very rich. Bush's proposal to create new savings accounts in which well-to-do families can put $60,000 that will *never* be taxed is a radical step to end taxation on wealth.[17] His slicing of the dividend tax is another huge giveaway to the rich, masquerading as a tax cut for all. And his massive income tax cuts, amounting to $10 trillion over 10 years, are a shameless bonanza for the wealthy. Under the Bush plan of 2002, the poorest 20 percent of the population in 2002 received an average income tax cut of $15. The middle 20 percent got an average cut of $170. The cut for the top 1 percent averaged $13,469. As for whether Bush's overall tax-cut plan offers compassion for the ordinary worker, secretary Luwaunna Adams, a Pennsylvania mother who makes $20,400 a year, got a tax benefit of $117 a year, or $2 a week. She appeared in a press conference with New Jersey millionaire senator Jon Corzine, who said he would get an annual tax benefit from Bush's plan of $1 million.[18]

The Democrats illustrated this huge gift to the rich when Democratic leaders Richard Gephardt, House minority leader, and Tom Daschle, Senate minority leader, appeared on Capitol Hill with a black Lexus sedan and an old, beat-up replacement muffler. Senator Daschle said that the car "was just like the Bush tax cut—fully loaded. If you're a millionaire, under the

Bush tax cut, you get a $46,000 tax cut, more than enough to pay for this Lexus. But if you're a typical working person, you get $227, and that's enough to buy this muffler."[19]

The wilding dimension of the tax cuts has been highlighted, ironically, by outspoken opposition to Bush's plan from some of the world's most famous billionaires. Warren Buffet, the nation's fourth-richest person; George Soros, the world's premier global investor; and William H. Gates Sr., head of the Gates Foundation and father of Bill Gates, joined dozens of other super-rich individuals attacking the Bush plan. They zeroed in on Bush's proposal to repeal the estate, or "death," tax. Gates Sr. says that "repealing the estate tax would enrich the heirs of America's millionaires and billionaires while hurting families who struggle to make ends meet." Buffet said Bush's plan "would be a terrible mistake," the same as "choosing the 2020 Olympic team by picking the eldest sons of the gold-medal winners in the 2000 Olympics. . . . Without the estate tax," Buffet concluded, "you in effect will have an aristocracy of wealth, which means you pass down the ability to command the resources of the nation based on heredity rather than merit."[20]

In fact, only 2 percent of the richest Americans pay the estate tax and would thus receive all the benefits of the repeal. Bush's own new head of faith-based giving, John J. DiIulio, Jr., has himself opposed repeal, since he agrees that the net effect would be to undermine the tax's financial incentive for charitable giving.[21]

It is interesting that in the one area in which Bush appears to have a genuine interest—improving education—he has proposed a modest increase in federal funding. Where the compassion is real, he retreats from his general hostility to public social spending. But even in education, the increase he proposes is, by virtually every expert account, so small that it will have little effect. While papered over by softer rhetoric, Bush's hostility to government is very clear in the details of his budget.

Making government the enemy has dangerous consequences. The right-wing terrorists who blew up the Alfred P. Murrah Federal Building in Oklahoma City on April 19, 1995, were influenced by a quarter-century of relentless attacks on government by politicians such as Ronald Reagan, Newt Gingrich, and Pat Robertson; talk-show radio personalities such as Rush Limbaugh; and the militant antigovernment ideologues who led the "patriot militias" of the 1990s. Convicted Oklahoma bomber Timothy J. McVeigh was not an isolated psychopath but a devoted disciple of extreme right-wing militia movements which have caught fire from Montana to Massachusetts. Such militias teach not only hatred of Jews, blacks, and immigrants, but a perverted individualism that sees driver's licenses, public schools, and Social Security cards as extreme infringements on personal freedom. They preach that government is the ultimate enemy of the people and should be demolished through bombings or other acts of sabotage of government installations. Militia militants, like McVeigh himself, are the bastard stepchildren of the conservative free-market fundamentalism that captured much of the nation in the 1980s and mid-1990s, and horrific wilding such as the Oklahoma City bombing will continue until the nation repudiates the antigovernment ideology that is the hallmark of the present era. Tax-cutting can serve the public interest only if it preserves the social infrastructure and protects the poor and middle class, who in the current tax revolution are paying more to support new business depreciation, capital gains, and offshore tax credits for the rich. As for government downsizing, the *New York Times*, noting that only 1 percent of the federal budget goes to welfare for the poor, proposes that human lives and much more money can be saved by slashing corporate welfare, including the billions of dollars now subsidizing agribusiness, oil, and mining industries and the billions more lost in outrageous business tax loopholes.

Environmentalists Jill Lancelot and Ralph De Genero suggest a "green scissors" approach to both tax-cutting and government pruning that would eliminate tax credits for companies and government programs that are ruining the environment at public expense. For starters, they suggest ending costly giveaway programs to the big mining corporations, such as the 1995 deal in which the Chevron and Manville corporations sought to pay $10,000 for national forest land in Montana estimated to be worth $4 billion in platinum deposits. To add insult to injury, such publicly subsidized mining deals lead to massive pollution, which ends up costing taxpayers an estimated $30 billion more to clean up.[22]

The assault on government is an intimate, perhaps suicidal, wilding dance between leaders and voters. Politicians and business conservatives are orchestrating the dance, according to Robert Kuttner, "channeling the raucous popular energy of the tax revolt into an orderly drive for systematic limitations on the welfare state and reductions in taxes on the well-to-do." The rich are using legitimate grievances by overtaxed homeowners and working people to reduce their own obligation to society. This proved to be such a fortuitous political recipe for the affluent that it has become the Bible of the Republican party; however, what has proved to be a guaranteed ticket to elected office may prove disastrous to society as a whole, for it is doubtful that a society can survive when those governing it become accessories to its breakdown.[23]

Ordinary voters are, at minimum, being willingly seduced to dance. Reporter John Powers argues that "cafeteria-style government is on the rise in Massachusetts as more taxpayers believe that they need pay only for what they order. Yes for plowing, no for schools. Hold the bridge repairs." Powers believes that Massachusetts voters may be breaking faith with their constitution, defined as "[a] social compact, by which the whole people covenants with each Citizen and each Citizen with the whole people." In the tax revolt, each voter is for himself or herself. Elderly and childless couples vote against raising taxes for schools. The young seek to ration health care for the elderly. And the well-to-do are prepared to cut back social services for the poor because in their eyes such programs are wasteful and create dependency. "Whatever happened," Powers asks, "to the common good?"[24]

Suzanne Gordon, an Arlington, Massachusetts, writer watching her neighbors acquiesce in the closing of one junior high school and two branch libraries, as well as the cutback of 30 percent of the city's workforce, sees the emergence of the "No Cares Cohort"—a "vast group of professionals between the ages of about twenty-five and forty. A lot of them don't have children till they're older, so they don't have to worry about taking care of them. They're young and healthy, so the disastrous decline in our health care system doesn't affect them. If they're married or living with someone, they're probably co-workaholics. . . . They are as removed from the social contract as those minority kids the system has truly abandoned." Gordon concludes that "our town is crumbling" because these residents are content to "sit idly by," with many "sucked into a swirl of antigovernment, antihuman frenzy. . . . The spirit of generosity seems to have been executed in Massachusetts, if not in the nation as a whole."[25]

Yet substantial majorities of taxpayers continue to tell pollsters they support earmarked spending for public universities, universal health care, and other specifically targeted social services, even as they vote against general tax increases, suggesting caution in proposing that voters have turned wholesale into mean-spirited Scrooges. Many voters say that they want to continue to help those truly in need but see government programs as a gigantic hoax and a waste, subsidizing bureaucrats rather than the poor. The public response is as much an attempt to deliver a swift kick to an overfed public bureaucracy as it is an abandonment of the needy.

My own interviews with about 30 Massachusetts voters suggest that suburbanites, affluent and geographically insulated from city life, most clearly fit the "mean-spirited" image. Many seem prepared to see the cities abandoned if their own comfortable lives could be preserved. The wilding ethos of the suburbs and the more affluent urban neighborhoods expresses itself less as a frenzied, "antihuman" rage than as an increasingly thick wall that makes the suffering of others emotionally tolerable. Most of the voters I interviewed believe that the larger society may be in danger of falling apart but find, nonetheless, a remarkable capacity to enjoy their own lives.

That a growing segment of the population is hell-bent on having a good time even as they recognize that the ship may be sinking is one of the most telling marks of the new wilding culture.[26]

Texan Justice: Political Wilding and the Prison–Industrial Complex

Presidents from Ronald Reagan to George W. Bush who have spearheaded the revolution against government are not telling you the truth. They do not really want to eliminate government because the capitalist economy and, especially, the superprofits of large corporations themselves depend on big government. When Ralph Nader ran for president in 2000, one of his main aims was to blast "corporate welfare"—the vast giveaways and subsidies doled out to big business. Without such help from "big government," corporate profits would rapidly decline.

The rich also need government to provide the police, prisons, and military security that protect them from the left-behinds both at home and abroad. As elites increase corporate welfare and use "trickle-up" tax policies to redistribute money to themselves, government leaders depend ever more on the use of force to contain the unrest of millions who languish in poverty, get downsized, and accumulate credit-card debt that threatens their ability to live the American Dream. In this section, we see that the massive increase in police and prisons reflects the effort to hold together by force a society that is deeply fractured by race and class.

State violence is political wilding when it involves the use of governmental force, for power or money, that ends up harming innocent people. State crime and violence have become a hot political topic in the new century. Nations around the world now seek to hold leaders accountable for war crimes, such as those of Serbia's deposed dictator, Slobodan Milosevic, who has been forced to appear before the International Court of Justice for genocidal campaigns of "ethnic cleansing." CIA coups against democratically elected foreign leaders, such as the one in 1973 that deposed Chile's president Salvador Allende, are another very important form of state violence that goes unpunished but constitutes egregious political wilding.[27]

The main concern here, though, is wilding practiced by our government at home. One prominent form is police brutality, symbolized most

famously by the beating of Rodney King, an African-American, that triggered the Los Angeles riots in the early 1990s. The tape of the King beating, replayed on television sets across the country, showed police officers hammering King 61 times in 87 seconds with metal batons, then continuing to kick and hit him as he lay face down and motionless on the ground. Struck initially by two police Taser darts carrying 50,000 volts of electricity each, King suffered a broken leg and several broken bones in his face.

Police brutality is just one expression of an epidemic of U.S. government violence against its own citizens, especially the poor, minorities, and immigrants. Sociologist Max Weber wrote that the state can be defined as the institution vested with a monopoly of the tools of official violence, including the military, police, courts, and prisons. When governments resort to police and prisons to repress racial minorities or disadvantaged groups, or to inflict excessively harsh force against any citizens (as in the famous Waco tragedy), they commit political wilding.

The movement of George W. Bush from the Texas governorship to the U.S. presidency has focused attention on the huge expansion of and violence in the prison system in the last decade. When Bush was governor, Texas built more prisons and executed more people than any other state. "Texan justice" is seen by many as an oxymoron, since so many of the Texans locked up and killed are African-Americans, and so much cruelty and capriciousness is built into the system.

As governor, Bush approved the execution of Karla Faye Tucker, a confessed murderer who had undergone a deep religious conversion and been a model prisoner for two decades. Supported by thousands of religious and other civic leaders, Tucker, a national symptom of redemption and humility, sought Bush's pardon. As was reported by conservative journalist Tucker Carlson for the debut of *Talk* magazine in 1999, Bush mocked Karla Faye's request for pardon by making a face and imitating her alleged despondency.

During the presidential debates, a spectator asked Bush if he was proud of all the executions he oversaw, and Bush said no. But many were looking for a more thoughtful response. The death penalty is outlawed in every European nation, and many Europeans' first reaction to Bush's election involved commentary about the barbarism of state execution and shock that Bush, as a symbol of American cruelty, had been elected.

In 2000, after a prisoner sentenced to death was proved innocent by DNA tests, the Republican governor of Illinois, George Ryan, suspended all executions in his state. His bold action catalyzed similar decisions in other states, where public opinion has begun to turn against the death penalty as immoral, a position long held by the Catholic Church. Whether the death penalty itself constitutes political wilding can be debated. But most agree that sentencing to death potentially innocent people who lack the money for fair legal representation and who have not been proved guilty by DNA testing and multiple other checks is unjust state violence. Moreover, experts on Texas courts and prisons have generally concluded that these flaws are blatantly evident in the Texas system and in many of the executions supervised by Bush when he was governor.

The death penalty controversy is only the tip of a rapidly escalating crisis of the prison system. More than 2 million people in 2000 were locked up in U.S. prisons, the most of any nation in the world and eight times the number incarcerated in 1970. Of these 2 million, 70 percent are minorities and half are African-Americans. One of every eight black males between the ages of 18 and 24 is in jail. "A black man in the state of California," University of California professor Angela Davis tells us, "is five times more likely to be found in a prison cell than in one of the state colleges or universities."[28]

America can barely build prisons fast enough to meet the demand. Corporations have leapt into the breach, building and operating hundreds of new prisons in the fastest-growing industry in America. Critics such as Davis have begun talking about the new "prison–industrial system." The term connotes a new melding of economic and political wilding, in which racism and poverty help fuel the growth of a huge disadvantaged prison population and the attendant prison system that returns billions of dollars in profit to wealthy investors.[29]

The raging controversy about "racial profiling," in which police target minorities for random drug checks, shows that wilding begins in the prison "recruitment" process. While African-Americans consume 13 percent of illegal drugs, they comprise 74 percent of the drug offenders sentenced to prison. This reflects not only racial profiling but also massive disparities in sentences for crack compared to powder cocaine, as well as police department drug-busting on urban streets rather than suburban parking lots. For most offenses, minorities are disproportionately likely to be arrested, sentenced, and physically abused by guards or denied medical treatment in jail.[30]

The prison–industrial system is not only racist but also class-biased, deeply punitive to the poor. White-collar and corporate criminals steal billions more than street burglars. Yet the percentage of corporate criminals who go to jail is far lower. The prison–industrial system returns fat profits to corporate criminals who should be incarcerated in the jails that make some of them rich. Much of the profit is extracted from prisoners forced to work for wages as low as 10 cents an hour.[31]

Wilding continues upon exit from the system, since many states deny released felons the right to vote and some illegally deny the franchise even to those convicted of misdemeanors. Fourteen percent of African-American men in the United States have lost their right to vote for alleged criminal offenses, and in some states the percentage is much higher. One-third of all black men in Alabama are disenfranchised, evoking memories of Jim Crow days and the slave South.[32]

The tortured Florida election count in 2000 puts a new light on these data. As Derrick Jackson writes, "In Florida, where Al Gore lost by 537 votes, 31 percent of African-American men, 200,000 of them, cannot vote because of felony convictions. For the Florida Republican Party, that was not enough. They hired a firm to purge the rolls even more, wrongly slashing thousands of people who were guilty only of misdemeanors."[33]

The 2000 presidential election, especially as played out in the Florida recount farce, is a case of one form of political wilding multiplied by another. At the very peak of the U.S. internal security system, which includes the judiciary as well as the prison–industrial complex, sits the Supreme Court. Bush ultimately became president because five members of the Supreme Court ruled that the Florida recount could not continue. Dissenters on the Court and hundreds of law professors have decried the decision as a historic stain on the entire judicial system.

The slim Supreme Court majority ruled that variation in counting methods in different Florida counties constituted a violation of the Fourteenth Amendment's equal-protection clause, originally passed, ironically, to protect the citizenship rights of freed slaves. But former Los Angeles deputy district attorney Vincent Bugliosi notes that "varying voting methods have been in use for two centuries; the Court has never hinted there might be a right that was being violated." Bugliosi's conclusion is stark. "These five justices," he writes, referring to the bare majority who ruled for Bush, "are criminals in every true sense of the word, and in a fair and just world belong behind prison bars." Even if one rejects Bugliosi's conclusion, there is the undeniable hint that judicial partisanship among the nation's highest judges subverted the will of the American people in electing a president. It is hard to imagine a more serious and frightening form of political wilding.[34]

War and Wilding

Iraq and the War against Terrorism

The great sociologist Max Weber defined the state as the institution with a monopoly of official violence, and Hans Morganthau, the famous political theorist, argued that states always act in their own self-interest. If states use their monopolies of violence to wage war for naked self-interest or corporate profits, this would appear to make war one of the most catastrophic forms of institutional wilding. We have already defined state violence for greed or power at home as political wilding, and in a world exploding with war for power and profit, it is hard to imagine a more dangerous and sociologically important species of wilding.

In this chapter, we consider two American wars: the war against Iraq and the "war on terrorism." In focusing on American-led wars, it is important to keep in mind that the United States is the greatest military power in world history and the sole superpower today. The U.S. spends more on the military—approaching half a trillion dollars annually—than all the other nations of the world combined. Many view the U.S. as an empire, exceeding in its power even the Roman or British empires. Sociologists such as Immanual Wallerstein and Giovanni Arrighi offer a framework known as "world system theory" for understanding the American empire as a wilding system. Looking back on the last 500 years of colonialism, world system theorists argue that the world economy has been organized by a dominant or "hegemonic" power, such as Britain during the late eighteenth and nineteenth centuries, that ruled over much of the world for profit and glory. The U.S. is the successor hegemon to Britain, with even greater power.[1]

Hegemony, as conceived by the Italian social theorist, Antonio Gramsci, is power dressed up in universal values such as freedom and prosperity. Gramsci wrote that governments always use such soothing rhetoric as "the white man's burden" to "manufacture consent," since naked coercion is an expensive and inefficient mode of control. During the British empire, the British claimed to bring civilization to the whole world, as did the ancient Romans to their conquered provinces. During the Cold War, the United States claimed to defend the entire "free world" against the evil of communism. Arrighi and other world system theorists observe that with the collapse of the Soviet Union, American hegemony is increasingly organized around claims to defend the whole civilized world against the evils of terror and chaos.

Hegemons increasingly turn to military force when their economic power and legitimacy begin to wane. The U.S. is in the early phases of hegemonic decline, associated with a long-term crisis in the global economy and the rise of a speculative "casino capitalism" that yields short-term profits at the expense of long-term growth. We can expect that the U.S. may move toward increasing militarism to secure its endangered global wealth and power, leading to the kind of mayhem and wilding witnessed during the decline and fall of the Roman and British empires.[2]

War in Iraq

When Baghdad fell on April 9, 2003, U.S. newspapers and television showed jubilant Iraqis dancing in the streets. Iraqis embraced and kissed American soldiers, stomped on pictures of Saddam Hussein, and with the help of U.S. Marines, toppled the huge iron statue of Saddam in central Baghdad. This was the reaction that President Bush had promised. Although no weapons of mass destruction had been found at this point, the Iraqi celebration seemed to nail down Bush's claim that this was a war of liberation, a just war destroying a barbaric regime and bringing freedom and democracy to a suffering nation.

As I write these words just after Baghdad's collapse, surveys suggest that most Americans agreed with the president. A poll released on April 10, 2003, showed that about 75 percent of Americans supported the war. Even those who had earlier protested the war were rethinking their opposition, wondering whether the end of a horrific despot justified the destruction inevitably wrought by war. One thoughtful student in my class raised his hand and said that the obvious joy of many Iraqis at the downfall of Saddam made him question whether his earlier opposition to the war was ignorant.

But while Americans watched images of Iraqis celebrating in the streets, Arabs were opening newspapers with headlines blazing "Humiliation!" and "Colonialism Is Back!" The images Arabs saw were of dead Iraqi children killed by bombs, starving Iraqi families screaming at U.S. soldiers for water or food, Iraqi soldiers lying dead on the highway, hospitals without electricity or medicine overflowing with wounded Iraqi civilians, widespread looting and mayhem, and fires burning out of control in many Iraqi cities. While there was no love lost on Saddam Hussein, Arabs all over the Mideast were horrified at the prospect of an American military occupation of Iraq.

Talal Salman, publisher of *Al-Safir*, a leading Lebanese moderate newspaper, grieved the loss of the richest Arab civilization to a "colonial power." Iraqis, he wrote, are now moving from "the night of tyranny" under Saddam Hussein to the "night of foreign occupation" under U.S. troops.[3] Ahmed Kamal Aboulmagd, a leading pro-Western member of the Egyptian establishment and a longtime friend of the U.S., said, "Under the present conditions, I cannot think of defending the United States. To most people in this area, the United States is the source of evil on planet earth."[4]

These sentiments were shared by many Iraqis, who were grateful to the U.S. and British soldiers for ousting Saddam but desperate to survive in the wake of the world's most intense bombing campaigns, and viscerally hostile to a new foreign occupation. The majority Shiite population in Iraq mounted huge street protests demanding that American soldiers get out of their country. Iraqis interviewed in Baghdad and Basra told U.S. reporters that they hated Saddam but they equally "resented the foreign troop presence." One Iraqi Shiite cleric said the Iraqis were caught between "two fires"—one, the cruel, fading power of Sadddam and the other the looming domination of the Americans. Qabil Khazzal Jumaa, an Iraqi nurse, horrified by the amputated limbs, burned bodies, and rotting corpses among the hundred of civilians he had treated, said that this was "a brutal war. This is not just. This is not accepted by man or God." Iraq did not belong to the Americans who would now govern his country. He said simply, "This is my country."[5]

In the face of these starkly competing images—Iraqis dancing in the streets and a bombed, looted country fearing subjugation to a hegemon occupying its cities and oil fields—how does one decide whether the U.S. war in Iraq was wilding? We can start by asking whether the war was legal and then whether this was a just war. This can be framed from a sociological perspective around the question of hegemony: did the U.S. invade Iraq to tighten its hegemonic control over the Gulf and the entire oil-rich Islamic world?

Legality

According to Article 51 of the U.N. charter (which the U.S. ratified), a country can legally engage in war without U.N. approval if the war is in self-defense. Right after 9/11, on September 12, 2001, President Bush redefined "self-defense" in a more expansive way than the charter implied. Bush asserted that the U.S. could no longer afford to abide by conventional concepts in an age of terrorism. We must be prepared, the president declared, "to strike at moment's notice in any dark corner of the world . . . to be ready for preemptive action when necessary to defend our liberty and to defend our lives." The president was very explicit about preemption: "We must take the battle to the enemy, disrupt his plans and confront the worst threats before they emerge."

In emphasizing that he would act against threats "before they emerge," the president was moving beyond preemption to prevention. A preemptive war occurs when a threat is imminent, for instance, when missiles or planes are detected moving toward one's shores, and there is a plausible concept of "pre-emptive self-defense" within the U.N.'s legal intent. Preventive war is a response to threats not yet visible, and suggests that one nation can use the new Bush doctrine to attack almost any other country that it mistrusts, an application of the wilding precept that "might makes right."

Bush's approach kicked up a firestorm of opposition. Former White House advisor William A. Galston said that Bush's new doctrine "means the end of the system of international institutions, laws, and norms that the United States has worked for more than half a century to build. . . . Rather than continuing to serve as first among equals in the postwar international system, the United States would act as a law unto itself, creating new rules of international engagement without agreement by other nations." Princeton political scientist Richard Falk, a leading authority on international law, writes that "this new approach repudiates the core of the United Nations charter [outlawing wars that are not based on self-defense against overt aggression] . . . it is a doctrine without limits, without accountability to the U.N. or international law, or any dependence on a collective judgment of responsible governments."[6]

When the U.S. invaded Iraq, it claimed that Article 51 made the war legal. The U.N. Security Council disagreed, saying that there was more time for inspection and that the threat was not imminent, meaning that the war could not be viewed as self-defense. France and Germany, along with scores of other countries, repeatedly argued that the war undermined the U.N. charter. Russian President Vladmir Putin declared that the doctrine of preemption meant the world would descend into chronic war and the law of the jungle.

Just a few weeks after Putin's prophecy of a new global anarchy, the government of India announced that it was using the Bush doctrine to consider a preemptive attack against its nuclear-armed adversary, Pakistan, because of Pakistan's incursions into the Indian-controlled part of Kashmir. A central problem with the invasion of Iraq—and the legal doctrine on which it is based—is that it offers a wilding license for international chaos.

Several months after the fall of Baghdad, American forces on the ground had failed to find any nuclear, biological, or chemical weapons. On April 24, 2003, President Bush suggested that weapons of mass destruction (WMD) might never be found and might not exist, raising grave new questions about the legality of the war. The president's legal argument for the war had rested on the premise that such weapons existed and constituted a threat to American and global security. But if no weapons are found, there was no threat and no plausible legal justification, suggesting a war of aggression rather than self-defense.[7]

Whether the president or other members of his administration lied about WMD or about Saddam's relation to Al Qaeda has become a major wilding issue in itself. Lying to create a legal justification for war would be political wilding of the highest order, and widespread suspicion of it has already inspired a mass campaign to impeach Bush led by former Attorney General Ramsey Clark. John Dean, President Nixon's legal advisor during Watergate, has said that if Bush lied about WMD, which he sees as more likely than any other explanation of the failure to find WMD in Iraq, it would be a far more serious impeachable offense than Nixon's cover-up in Watergate. "In the three decades since Watergate," Dean wrote, "this is the first potential scandal I have seen that could make Watergate pale by comparison. . . . To put it bluntly, if Bush has taken Congress and the nation into war based on bogus information, he is cooked. Manipulation or deliberate misuse of national security intelligence data, if proven, could be a 'high crime' under the Constitution's impeachment clause."[8]

In his 2003 State of the Union message, President Bush claimed that Iraq had 30,000 warheads and the materials to produce 38,000 liters of botulinum toxin, 25,000 liters of anthrax, and 500 tons of chemical weapons, none of which have been found at this writing. Bush also told the American public in the State of the Union that Iraq tried to buy uranium from the African country of Niger, even though CIA officials had earlier told Vice President Cheney's office and Bush's National Security Council that the Niger story was an obvious fabrication based on forged documents. The White House acknowledged in July 2003 that Bush should not have included the unfounded allegation about Niger in his speech.[9] The specter of a pattern of lying to create the impression that Iraq posed a nuclear threat is reinforced by Bush's public claim that aluminum tubes in Iraq's possession were intended to enrich uranium after the International Atomic Energy Agency had already publicly concluded that the tubes probably had nothing at all to do with a nuclear program. Bush also claimed that Saddam Hussein was supporting Al Qaeda, when both his own intelligence agencies and the U.N. reported little evidence of this. Bush's statements have led up to 50 percent of Americans to say that they believe that Saddam was behind 9/11, suggesting that Americans were all too ready to believe a president who repeatedly misled them.

One explanation is the soft-pedaling by American media and Congress itself about the official pattern of deception, itself a dangerous form of wilding. In Britain, where the media outrage and public anger have been hotter, two leading cabinet ministers resigned after the Iraqi war, accusing Prime Minister Blair of lying to Britons about WMD. One of the resigning ministers, Claire Short, testified to a parliamentary committee that Blair and Bush concocted a prearranged deal in 2002 to invade Iraq in 2003 no matter what was found about weapons of mass destruction. Blair, at this writing, faces several fierce parliamentary investigations and hardhitting major media attacks accusing him of lying. But while the *New York Times* headlined the question "Was the intelligence cooked?" the *Times* and other media, as well as the American Congress, have expressed little outrage about the pattern of official deception and the political manipulation of intelligence data. When Vice President Cheney was reported to have walked over to the CIA and spent hours grilling intelligence officials involved with Iraq and other American intelligence officials have disclosed that they felt pressure to come up with results favorable to the administration's case for war, the media gave it little attention. Such political pressure on intelligence analysts, if true, is a horrific form of political wilding, undermining the credibility of the president and endangering democracy, just as the pressure by Wall Street firms on analysts for favorable stock reports endangers the credibility and future of the financial markets. By failing to focus the American public on Bush's distortions and suspected lies that served his war interests, the media have helped normalize such official deception and contributed to a culture of political wilding that has severely damaged our country.

Justice

The question of wilding goes beyond legality to the broader issue of whether the war on Iraq was a just war of liberation. While the argument that the removal of a tryant is indeed a just action is true, three arguments based on historical, economic, and political perspectives suggest other goals were behind this war.

The historical argument is based on planning documents only recently made public. In a 1990 strategy document put together by a team under Dick Cheney in the first Bush administration, the United States announced that it must "preclude the rise of another global rival for the indefinite future," building such an overwhelming military superiority that no other nation could possibly contemplate challenging American power. The Cheney document suggested that the United States needed to create a "democratic zone of peace" in which Americans would be prepared to use force if necessary to ensure "human rights or democracy," even if using force involved violating the sovereignty of another nation that posed no threat to the United States. While Iraq was the test case of the time, the idea of overthrowing Saddam was rejected after the first Gulf War because the U.N. did not authorize a regime change. The Cheney doctrine was shelved as embarrassingly imperialistic.[10] Nonetheless, after 9/11, Cheney's vision became the centerpiece of the new Bush administration's foreign policy, and the Iraqi war was a crucial first step toward securing the global dominance laid out in the earlier documentary record.[11]

A second argument that the war on Iraq involved wilding centers around the economic goals of the war. Like all prior hegemons, the United States has two economic agendas. The first is to ensure the stable operation of the world economy, including the guarantee of a cheap supply of Mideast oil. In 1990, when Saddam Hussein invaded Kuwait and threatened Saudi Arabia, the United States launched the first Gulf War to stabilize the entire global economic system, protecting the oil supply not only for itself but for European and Asian allies. In the 2003 Gulf War, the United States again acted with broad concern for global economic stability based on securing greater control of Iraq's and its neighbors' oil supplies—still a form of wilding but different than simply grabbing more profit for U.S. oil companies.

Another U.S. economic aim, though, is closer to what the protestors had in mind as they waved their "No Blood for Oil" signs. The corporatized American hegemon sees U.S. national interests as tightly connected to the profitability of politically influential American corporations. The Bush administration, including most notably the president and vice president, is especially close to the energy industries, in which several Bush cabinet members served as corporate executives, as well as to the military-related companies rooted in Texas and throughout the Southwest of the United States. It is predictable that the interests of this sector of American corporations would weigh heavily in the Bush administration's assessment of the national interest.

Evidence that profits for U.S. oil giants and other companies were part of the Iraq war aim comes from the postwar reconstruction contracts, which the U.S. Agency for International Development has begun to award through a closed bidding process.

- Halliburton, the Texas-based oil giant formerly headed by Dick Cheney, was awarded the first major contract for servicing of Iraqi oil wells and fire prevention in the oil fields, estimated to be worth up to $7 billion. This is widely seen as a foot in the door for more profitable long-term Iraqi oil contracts, and has led to discussions of a congressional investigation regarding whether Halliburton poses a conflict of interest, since Cheney still receives compensation from the firm.

- The United States has also awarded a leading reconstruction role to Bechtel, the vast construction and energy company with ties to Secretary of Defense Donald Rumsfeld and others closely connected to the Bush administration. George Schultz, former president of Bechtel and currently on its board, also sits on Bush's Pentagon's Defense Policy Board, which advises the administration about Iraq and other vital matters. Richard Perle, head of that same board and the leading hawk on Iraq, was forced to resign his chairmanship when concerns about potential conflicts of interest were raised about his own business interests. At a time when Pentagon planners and the CIA were predicting major new terrorist attacks as a near certainty in the wake of the Iraqi invasion, Perle's company stood to generate lucrative profits from defense and homeland security contracts.[12]

A third argument that the Iraqi war involved wilding concerns domestic political benefits reaped by the Bush administration. Bush entered office without a popular majority and only through a controversial Supreme Court decision about the Florida vote. Even before 9/11 and the Iraq war, critics perceived Bush as a servant of the big corporations whose campaign funding had helped propel him to Washington. In his first moves as president, Bush chose a cabinet led by other former corporate executives, including Cheney, Rumsfeld, and Paul O'Neill, his Secretary of the Treasury. Bush then pushed a domestic agenda centered around the biggest tax cuts to the rich in history, enhancing his image as a political stand-in for his corporate friends.

Such a corporate presidency is inherently vulnerable to a crisis of legitimacy. Bush's social and economic domestic policies have been consistently opposed by a majority of the American electorate. Karl Rove, the president's political guru, has denied in public that foreign policy decisions are made on the basis of domestic political considerations, but he sent a secret memo to Republican activists during the 2002 midterm elections urging them to "focus on the war." He also acknowledged to reporters during the 2002 campaign that he liked the slogan circulating among Republican strategists, "Are you safer now than you were four years ago?"[13]

The domestic political benefits of war in Iraq are too obvious to ignore. While a majority of Americans in polls continue to say they worry about the economy and feel that Bush's domestic agenda is moving the country in the wrong direction, Bush's poll numbers spiked up after the fall of Baghdad. Leaders with unpopular domestic policies have frequently turned to war as a way of countering their slide in the polls, and wars have typically helped presidents regain popularity in the wake of economic downturns. Reliance on war to divert the public from domestic problems has been dubbed the "wag the dog" strategy, and has been widely discussed ever since the popular movie of the same title was made. If even a small part of the Iraq war was driven by political concerns about re-election, this would be a devastating indictment of the war as wilding.

The War on Terrorism

9/11 was a watershed event. When Al Qaeda operatives hijacked the two jumbo jets and crashed them into the twin towers in New York, they showed that the U.S. was vulnerable to the devastating violence that many other countries have suffered for decades. Americans have historically felt protected by the oceans and the enormous power of the U.S. military. We know now that tiny bands of terrorists can inflict horrific damage on our country, whatever the size of our military or our hegemonic power.

Is the American-led war on terrorism a form of wilding? If it is truly an international struggle to eradicate groups such as Al Qaeda, then diplomatic, police, intelligence, and military actions designed for such aims may be morally legitimate. But the history of hegemonic powers—and of the

U.S. in particular—offers cautions. During the Cold War, many wars fought in the name of anticommunism, such as the 1954 overthrow of Guatemela's elected president Jacobo Arbenz, had more to do with protecting the United Fruit Company's banana plantations than fighting Communism. The 1953 CIA overthrow of another democratically elected leader, Iran's President Mohammed Mossadegh, was also an imperialist war. It was called an anticommunist war, but was waged mainly to protect U.S. oil interests. The Cold War developed into a form of hegemonic wilding, involving scores of greed- and power-driven military interventions by the U.S. to build the American empire as well as wars by the Soviet Union to build its own empire.[14]

During the period of Roman hegemonic decline, in the fourth and fifth centuries A.D., the rise of terror from the invading Germanic tribes became a central security issue on the Roman empire's eroding boundaries. Similarly, as the British empire declined, it faced terrorist attacks from African colonies such as Kenya, as well as nationalist attacks from groups such as the Zionists in Israel. If the U.S. is entering a period of hegemonic decline, then we might expect not only disorder and terrorism but a "war on terrorism" that is entirely predictable, since many declining hegemons have waged such a war to preserve their dominance.

What, then, are the real motives driving the war on terrorism that began after 9/11? One is undoubtedly to destroy Al Qaeda and similar violent, criminal groups, and if this were its sole purpose, directed and carried out by the U.N. in coalition with the U.S., the war would not be wilding. But just as the Soviet threat served a useful function for American leaders during the Cold War, the threat of terrorism helps U.S. elites achieve their aims. In fact, the U.S. and its terrorist enemies function like spouses in a long and hostile co-dependent marriage. They hate each other but need the marriage because it serves crucial functions for each of them. While trying to destroy one another, they also become increasingly reliant on the conflict between them to survive and achieve their own aims.

A key codependent marriage has developed between the U.S. elites and Al Qaeda. Both seek to destroy the other, but at the same time find each other exceedingly useful in promoting their own ends. The American empire provides Al Qaeda with its most potent tool for rallying Arab popular support and undercutting moderate Islamic groups that could make the radicals irrelevant. Similarly, Al Qaeda offers American political leaders their most powerful case for vastly enhanced military spending and wars that bring profit, power, and political legitimacy at home.

A major covert aim of the war on terrorism is to replace the war on communism in order to build the American empire and stem the global tide of anti-Americanism. Put simply, terrorism (and the war against it) has become a powerful selling point for the global wilding policies at the heart of empire. Without Al Qaeda, the Bush administration could not have diverted so much money to expanding the armed forces, especially in an era of decline in jobs and domestic social services. Nor could U.S. leaders have explicitly proclaimed the doctrines of preemptive war and unrivalled military dominance. Al Qaeda has provided U.S. leaders with an argument to introduce American forces in scores of countries as well as to overthrow governments that have not attacked the U.S., which is perhaps the defining feature of an imperial power. Without their hated terrorist partners, American leaders could not have attacked Iraq, by falsely linking Saddam Hussein with Al Qaeda, or pursued so blatantly the new politics of preventive war and empire.

Another unacknowledged aim of the war on terrorism, also suggestive of systemic political wilding, has been to increase the political standing of the president at home. As noted earlier, President Bush heads a corporate state. He has not only proposed huge tax cuts for the rich but increased subsidies for agribusiness, pharmaceuticals, and other big industries; he has proposed drilling in the Alaskan wilderness and other energy policies that were a bonanza for the biggest energy giants; and he has supported deregulation that would enrich telecom, mining, and nearly every other corporate sector. This has not played well with the American public. By early 2003, as corporations celebrated the new gifts coming from Washington, half of Americans worried that they might not have a job in a year. Many saw their pension nest eggs vanishing, while access to basic health care and education drastically eroded.

The war on terrorism was the answer to the political problem posed by the inevitable public opposition to the domestic agenda of the corporate state. Bush's political vulnerability at home would be shared by any president, Democrat or Republican, who presided over the corporate state, since such a government is structurally committed to policies that do not benefit the majority of Americans. If new corporate presidents continue to rely on the war on terrorism for their political survival, we may be faced with one wilding war after another, fought in the name of anti-terrorism, for political benefits at home. After the fall of Baghdad, rumors surfaced almost immediately of new potential confrontations with Syria, North Korea, and Iran. Fighting even one war for domestic political gain is a horrific form of political wilding; fighting a whole generation of such wars is systemic wilding on a grand scale.

Nations around the world *do* need to come together to try to prevent terrorism. It is precisely because the threat is real and frightening that it is such a powerful tool for manipulating public opinion. In the face of a very real threat, we need a more effective and honest approach to stopping terrorism. What would such an approach look like? First, it would be directed by the United Nations and the international community rather than by the United States. Second, it would attack the root causes of terrorism, requiring major changes in U.S. foreign and economic policy. This would include a far more balanced American approach to the Israeli-Palestinian conflict, the most explosive issue in the Middle East. The U.S. could do more to end terror by pushing Israel to ending illegal settlements and accept a viable Palestinian state than by taking any other step, since this would dry up support for Hamas and other Palestinian extremist groups. This will require more pressure on Israel than Bush has exercised since his introduction of his Roadmap to Peace, which most Palestinians correctly perceive as tilted to favor the Israelis. Ending U.S. military occupation of the region and withdrawing U.S. support for the brutal monarchies and sheikdoms there is also essential. This could take place only if the U.S. renounces its aspiration for global hegemony, acknowledging that empire is incompatible with its own democratic ideals as well as with global peace.

An effective anti-terror strategy would imply changing the rules of globalization—which is now the economic expression of American hegemony—such that poor people in the Middle East and around the world are not forced to bear the burden of debt while being denied the means to shape their own development policies. As long as the U.S. imposes a globalization that does not help the 3 billion people who eat fewer calories a day than the ordinary American's cat or dog, we are going to have more anti-American terror.

A war on terrorism that is not wilding would be political, economic, and diplomatic, rather than military. Police and other agents of coercive force may be required to root out violent groups, but the most effective way to do so requires enacting just global policies and involving the full cooperation of other nations and of publics all over the world. The war on terrorism is, of all wars, the one most dependent on winning the hearts and minds of the people.

Beyond Wilding

Resurrecting Civil Society

An injury to one is the concern of all.
—Knights of Labor motto

Wilding has taken a devastating toll on America, but it has not permanently incapacitated it. Societies, like individuals, have powerful natural resistance and a remarkable capacity to regenerate themselves. While Ik society was destroyed, America, always resilient, has far greater economic and cultural resources to revitalize itself. To succeed, however, it will have to focus all its efforts on the task, which involves shoring up the ideal of a "civil society" at its very foundations.

Creating and supporting a civil society is the underlying antidote to the wilding virus, involving a culture of love, morality, and trust that leads people to care for one another and for the larger community. A civil society's institutions nurture civic responsibility by providing incentives for people to act not just in their own interest but for the common good. Governments must provide a supportive framework, but a robust civil society cannot be legislated. It must arise from the cooperation and moral sensibilities of ordinary people who understand that their own fulfillment requires thriving communities and an intact society.

Reflections on civil society date back to Aristotle but have been revisited in modern times following the cataclysmic changes in Eastern Europe and the Soviet Union. The dictatorial governments that ruled for decades in the name of communism systematically undermined civil society, crushing all independent groups or communities that resisted their rule. As the people, already suffering from preexisting ethnic and nationalist conflicts, became increasingly atomized, unable to trust either their governments or their fellow citizens, a wilding culture emerged. It remained largely invisible, held in check by the all-powerful authorities. But after 1989, with the collapse of the Berlin Wall and the government it symbolized, the wilding forces that had been suppressed for so many years were now free to surface. An epidemic erupted in the form of revived anti-Semitism, with other ethnic and ultranationalist poisons spreading through the region, including the horrific "ethnic cleansing" in Bosnia and Kosovo. After the initial revolutionary euphoria had worn off, civic indifference, apathy, and a lack of trust and cooperation developed among citizens. Calls for the resurrection of civil society have reverberated from Budapest and Prague to Moscow. Some leaders, such as Czech Republic president Vaclav Havel, recognize that the biggest challenge after decades of rule under the rhetoric of collectivism, is, ironically, the rebuilding of community.

The wilding crises in Eastern Europe and the United States are different from one another; one was bred by coercive collectivism and the other by untrammeled free-market individualism. Sociologist Alan Wolfe writes that both an overreaching government and an overblown market can, in different ways, colonize civil society and destroy it—the market, by glorifying selfishness, and the state, by substituting paternalism or coercion for conscience. Civil society blooms only where markets and governments are kept in reasonable check, and families, communities, and voluntary associations, the institutional seedbeds of love, morality, and trust, are free to prosper. The bonds of conscience and caring, as well as mechanisms of social accountability discussed below, help ensure that private interests do not override the common good.[1]

Although there is no magic formula and no perfect model, civil society is the strongest and most suitable medicine for the wilding epidemic. Americans now must urgently recognize that they need to dedicate themselves unwaveringly to reconstructing their society.

The Case for Hope

More than 150 years ago, Alexis de Tocqueville worried that America was vulnerable to an individualism that "saps the virtues of public life" and "in the long run" might "attack and destroy" society itself. Tocqueville described it as an individualism "which disposes each member of the community to sever himself from the mass of his fellows," and to "feel no longer bound by a common interest." Americans must always be on guard, Tocqueville advised, against the deterioration of their individualistic culture into "a passionate and exaggerated love of self, which leads a man to connect everything with himself, and to prefer himself to everything else in the world."[2]

Tocqueville did not disapprove of the healthy self-interest that energized Americans, but he saw the thin line separating American individualism from wilding. Without strongly developed moral codes, the restless pursuit of self-interest inherent in a market economy could at any time degrade into an egoistic menace that might destroy society. But Tocqueville, a sober observer, was also extraordinarily optimistic about the American experiment. Counteracting the wilding virus was another side of America, the strength of its civil society. One manifestation was the personal generosity and helpfulness that he observed in all his American travels. "Although private interest directs the greater part of human actions in the United States," Tocqueville wrote, "it does not regulate them all. I must say that I have often seen Americans make great and real sacrifices to the public welfare; and I have remarked a hundred instances in which they hardly ever failed to lend faithful support to each other." Because an American is neither master nor slave to his fellow creature, "his heart readily leans to the side of kindness."[3]

Tocqueville recognized that the kinder and gentler side of American life was grounded in the political rights and free institutions that "remind every citizen, and in a thousand ways, that he lives in society." Tocqueville marveled at Americans' propensity to "constantly form associations" of a thousand kinds in which they "voluntarily learn to help each other." Americans were constantly connecting and spontaneously creating the bonds of friendship, trust, and cooperation that lie at the heart of civil society.[4]

In the century and a half since Tocqueville's visit, the wilding epidemic has spread throughout America, but it has not totally destroyed the civil society that made such an impression on him. Much evidence suggests that Americans retain some of the openness, generosity, and moral idealism that, in Tocqueville's view, differentiated them from Europeans. Likewise, the free institutions and "propensity to associate" have not vanished. It is the sturdiness of this base, its survival in the face of the wilding onslaught, that offers grounds for optimism and a direction for the future.

Each year in Boston, more than 50,000 people join the Walk for Hunger. The marchers hike for 20 miles, often in inclement weather, to raise money for Project Bread, a group that helps provide meals for the homeless and hungry. Each participant takes time to approach sponsors, who agree to donate a certain amount of money for each mile that the walker completes. As one curbside viewer said, "You've got the elderly walking, you've got kids walking, you've got families walking. To me, it's the most beautiful sight to see all the people walking." Such walks are only one in a cornucopia of charitable endeavors that regularly take place in cities and towns across the United States.

At the very time that taxpayers are revolting and turning off the public spigot, volunteers are stepping in to help stop the shortfall that their own votes have precipitated. In many towns across the country, playground construction is done mainly by volunteers, in the spirit of traditional community barn-raising. In Plymouth, Massachusetts, the town library stays open only because of the generosity of more than 50 volunteers; in nearby Raynham, the school libraries are run entirely by volunteers. Community booster groups rally to raise money to keep public buildings painted, keep school sports programs going, and plant trees and maintain the city parks.[5]

Even in the heart of Wall Street there are signs of the other America. Several multimillionaire commodities traders created the Robin Hood Foundation, an offbeat center that scours New York City "looking for neighborhood foundations that rescue the homeless, care for children with AIDS, fight drug abuse, or rebuild families." The organization links community activists to business sponsors and technical experts who can be helpful. One of the founders says, "I couldn't sleep if I did not have a part in this sort of thing," and another says, "I love this city with a passion. I'm a walking poster for New York. I don't want to see the city go under."[6]

Such anecdotes are backed up by hard statistics documenting the generous side of America. About 7 out of every 10 households contribute to charity, donating an average of almost 2 percent of household income, a figure almost four times greater than that in Canada and England (a comparison that should take into account the national health plans and large social welfare programs that taxpayers in the latter countries support, thereby reducing the need for charity). About 45 percent of Americans over the age of 18 sacrifice their own time to volunteer, averaging about four hours a week and totaling almost 20 billion hours of volunteer time nationwide.[7]

How can the wilding epidemic spread at the same time that moral commitments and compassionate behavior persist at these levels? As I argued in Chapter 1, America is simultaneously host to a wilding culture and a civil culture, with sectors of the elites increasingly immersed in wilding and a vast number of ordinary Americans uneasily straddling the two cultures. Most Americans' lives are a struggle to reconcile wilding impulses with a nagging conscience that refuses to die. Many succumb to wilding pressures at the office but discover their humanity with family or friends. Conversely, some become wilders in their personal lives but express their conscience in admirable careers dedicated to constructive professional or business enterprise, public service, or social change.

The stubborn persistence of civil society and moral commitment provides a fertile seedbed for social reconstruction. The way to stop the wilding epidemic is to bolster all the empathic and moral sensibilities that

Americans already display. Although these need to be fortified and mobilized with new visions, the project is more akin to catalyzing the surviving
immune system of a weakened patient than transplanting a new immune
system to the patient whose own defenses have been destroyed.

But solving the problem will take serious cultural and institutional
change. As I have argued, wilding grows out of an American individualism that is deeply rooted. The country's leadership and major institutions
increasingly fuel Americans' wilding side and provide serious disincentives
to their less egoistic inclinations. We need the culture, economics, and
politics of a civil society, where the rules of success encourage attention
to morality and the common good. More precisely, we must rewrite the
rules of the game so that those who neglect the collective interest will not
prosper and those who take it into account will realize their just rewards.

Rethinking the American Dream: A New Communitarianism?

The American Dream has not always been a cultural template for wilding.
As we consider rewriting the Dream for a better future, we have the conso-
lation that we can look to our history for guidance. Through most of America's past, the purely materialistic and individualistic side of the Dream has
tended to be balanced by a moral and community-oriented side, preventing the Dream from transmuting into a wilding recipe. Moreover, the Dream
has been inclusive, defining a set of common purposes to which all Americans could aspire. These historical features of the Dream need to be recap-
tured in order to fortify civil society and purge the wilding epidemic.

The individualistic dream dominating today has its roots in the mythology of the self-made man and, as historian James Combs argues, "stems
from the ideology of capitalism and the myth of unlimited abundance."
The nineteenth-century novelist Horatio Alger immortalized the materialist Dream in his rags-to-riches fables. In its current form, it celebrates American heroes such as basketball superstar Michael Jordan, who rose to fab-
ulous success through his extraordinary individual talent and hard work.[8]

The materialistic dimensions of the Dream have become so dominant
that most Americans have forgotten that there was once another side to
the Dream. America has traditionally defined itself in terms of a set of high
moral ideals, including democracy, equality, and tolerance. Values grow-

ing out of the religious and political foundations of the country, including the Puritan zeal for community and the American Revolution's idealization of civil democracy, helped to shape another dream, one that mythologized family, community, and civic responsibility. Through most of American history, the materialistic dream prevailed, but the dream that elevated community values provided a warning that success should not be achieved at any price. America idealized its rural and small-town communities where, to a greater or lesser degree, as Combs notes, "religion, family, and democratic good feelings tempered the quest for power and money." Small-town community is still part of American mythology, which helps explain why President Clinton proudly publicized his roots in the town of Hope, Arkansas, and President Bush II speaks nostalgically of his boyhood in a tiny Texan town.[9]

The two dreams define a creative tension in American history. While at some times in our history, the materialistic dream prevailed, in the 1930s, the Great Depression mobilized Americans to rally together and fashion a collective lifeline to ride out the economic storm. President Franklin Delano Roosevelt reinvigorated the dream of moral community, using the government to affirm that in a time of desperate need, Americans would take care of each other. Three decades later, in the 1960s, a whole generation of youth plunged into social activism and communal experiments, seeking a morally attractive alternative to the materialist dream of their 1950s childhoods.

The failure of the aspirations of the 1960s has led, in the decades since then, to perhaps the most extensive subordination of the moral dream in American history. To purge the wilding epidemic, Americans in the twenty-first century will have to rediscover and refashion a version of the moral dream in order to temper the current fever of individualistic materialism and resurrect civil society.

The moral vision will have to be creative because of the new threats that unchecked materialism now poses. It will have to encompass an ecological morality, for we now know that the untrammeled materialist dream is incompatible with planetary survival, becoming a form of wilding directed against nature itself. Global warming—the catastrophic heating up of the earth through promiscuous use of fossil fuels—is only the most frightening of the legacies of such environmental wilding. If Americans cannot learn to live within the limits dictated by the environment, they will be engaged not only in crimes against nature but in a form of wilding against future generations who will bear the ultimate consequences.

Americans find it hard to accept any limits on materialism, for the dominant dream has equated freedom and fulfillment with the right to become as rich or famous as luck, talent, or hard work permits. To suggest that Bill

Gates should not have been allowed to make or keep the nearly $100 billion he now has strikes us as un-American. But a civil society must respect not only ecological limits but also those dictated by the traditional American morality of fair play and egalitarianism. Uncapping all limits in the recent orgy of greed and deregulation has polarized the country, creating an unprecedented and morally unbearable division between rich and poor.[10]

Civil society is a society of inclusion, and the new dream will have to script new trade-offs between individual freedom and the survival of the community. This ultimately requires reviving a moral dream of community; not the utopian vision of communes that failed in the 1960s, but something simultaneously more modest and more ambitious: a reawakening of the American sense of community that can mobilize the country to unify and preserve itself in an era of unprecedented division.

The Social Market: Sociological Sense and Dollars and Cents

As Americans have struggled to choose between the materialist dream and the moral dream, they have had to wrestle with the tensions between the free market and community. The market system is an excellent vehicle for delivering the promises of the materialist dream, but it is far less effective in preserving the moral fiber of society. In periods when the moral dream has come more strongly to the fore, as in the 1930s and 1960s, Americans have pioneered economic models, such as the New Deal and the Great Society, that depart from free-market scripture.

Europeans have spent an entire century building an alternative with a social conscience to the free market. The Swedes, Danes, Austrians, and Germans recognize that they are not playing Adam Smith's game. "We are not operating a marketplace economy," admits German industrialist Helmut Giesecke, but rather a "social marketplace economy [that] guarantees food, shelter, schooling, and medical attention to every person, not as welfare but as human rights." Government, labor, and business work together to reconcile prosperity with social justice. German business has supported this program, according to Giesecke, because "this social network really works," leading to a well-educated, healthy, and motivated workforce whose productivity keeps increasing.[11]

Perhaps ultimately the Germans support the social infrastructure because they know firsthand the horrific consequences when society totally breaks down. They have experienced a Germany gone completely wild, and many recognize that it could happen again. The greater internal homogeneity of Germany, Austria, Sweden, and other European "social market" societies also allows them to feel a greater connection to others and to savor the sense of family. Even as European cultures grow more individualistic and consumerist, their social marketplace economies may prevent a descent into wilding.

The development of an American social market could be one of the most potent remedies for the wilding epidemic. It would provide a way to reconcile economic growth and justice, and to help solve America's social problems by building on its own deepest value: democracy.

The social market is the economic recipe for a civil society, but the Western European version is not one Americans are likely to embrace. The European model is a universal welfare state, in which the government shelters groups unprotected by the market; responds to the medical, housing, and social needs of the population that the market neglects; and comprehensively regulates business to ensure social responsibility. But the record of American history, as well as its current fiscal crisis, argues against the likelihood that Americans, barring another Great Depression, will look solely to the state; although there is a crucial role for government to play in stopping the wilding epidemic, it can only be a catalyst, not the central player.

The key to a social market system is not big government but new institutions, whether public or private, that rectify the tendency of our current market economy to write social costs and benefits out of the equation. The American free market responds mainly to the desires of the individual actor—whether a person or corporation—and is largely indifferent to the spillover effects that transactions may have on the rest of society. When a factory decides to pollute, the social cost of bad air and ensuing discomfort or respiratory disease is what economists call an externality: a real cost, but one that the factory owner can ignore, because society, rather than the factory, pays the ultimate bill. In the pure free-market model, there is neither an economic incentive for the individual to help society nor a market disincentive to be antisocial; the market simply does not discriminate, operating with so-called benign neglect. As such neglect accumulates, with the market turning a blind eye to the millions of externalities that affect society every day, benign neglect becomes catastrophic social blindness and civil society is placed in jeopardy.

A social market corrects such social blindness by writing social costs and benefits back into the equation. It is a market that seeks to internalize the externalities, thus becoming socially responsible by giving social stakeholders a voice in corporate decisions and by devising strategies to guarantee that economic wilders pay the cost of their sociopathic behavior (and, conversely, that the good citizen will receive his or her just rewards). One way to create this social market is to rely on government, which can compel prosocial choices through legislation or induce them through tax incentives, as when the state enforces worker health and safety standards or gives tax credits to factories installing antipollution devices. But there is another approach, one equally appealing to Americans wary of government and committed to democracy, that involves redesigning economic institutions to be better equipped to exercise social responsibility on their own initiative. One such approach involves new corporate ownership and participation arrangements, in which workers and local citizens gain a voice and can speak up for the needs of the larger community. The Germans, although relying primarily on government, have also invented a "co-determination" system, which requires that every industrial enterprise with more than 500 workers select half its governing board of trustees from among its own employees. This has been successful for more than 40 years, contributing not only to the German economic boom but to a civil industrial society in which ordinary workers have been able to ensure that their health and safety are protected, their grievances addressed, and their jobs protected by investment strategies that prioritize domestic employment as well as overseas profit. Co-determination is a version of economic democracy that works.

Sociologist Severyn Bruyn describes the many down-to-earth ways, some already highly developed in America, to fashion a social market that works to dissuade economic wilding and preserve civil society without resorting to big government. Numerous forms of worker ownership and participation, including cooperatives and employee stock ownership plans (ESOPs), in which employees own a piece or all of their companies, can help compel companies to treat their employees fairly and practice workplace democracy. The cooperative, as its name implies, has the potential to turn the workplace itself into a civil society because everyone within it has equal rights and self-interest is more closely wedded to the collective interest than in a conventional firm. Another innovation involves corporate social charters that bind businesses to designated social missions, as in the case of community credit unions which are structured to reinvest in the community and offer low-interest loans to poorer residents. Land trusts—modern versions of the colonial concept of the commons—can remove property from the commercial market and legally

ensure that it is used to serve community needs. A new field of social accounting can help take stock of the social costs and benefits of corporate decisions. Social capital, such as the trillions of dollars in American
pension funds, one of the largest and still-growing pots of money in the
world, can be used to invest in affordable housing and community economic development. The new practice of social investing could be the
first step in turning the stock market into what sociologist Ritchie Lowry
calls "good money," where investors seek a profit but also a social return
on their money. "Social screens"—report cards on companies compiled
by outside analysts—now tell investors which corporations are economic
wilders and which are responsible citizens. Companies that want to at-
tract the funds of millions of social investors have to demonstrate not
only what they are doing for the bottom line but what they are doing
for their communities.[12]

America has not yet built a main highway toward this version of the
social market, but it is already carving out many smaller roads in that
direction. There are now more than 10 thousand American ESOPs, including huge companies such as United Airlines, Avis, and Weirton Steel,
and there is evidence that they are more responsive to their employees
and their customers. Studies show that worker-owners are more produc-
tive and deliver higher quality, with Avis now number one in ratings of
customer satisfaction. Hundreds of ESOPs and cooperatives, including large
worker-owned factories, practice sophisticated forms of workplace democracy. They are proving effective in job creation and retention, and are responsible for saving hundreds of jobs during the epidemic of factory clos-
ings in the last decade. According to polls, including one by Peter Hart,
economic democracy makes sense to most Americans; approximately 70
percent say that they would welcome the opportunity to work in an
employee-owned company.[13]

The thousand American companies with the highest percentage of employee ownership constitute the nucleus of a new social market sector of
the economy. The proliferation of 401K retirement plans, in which workers receive pension benefits in the form of employee stocks, can be risky
for workers, but will increase the size and power of this new economic sector. If these companies sustain employee loyalty, high productivity, and
robust profits, they will teach a much wider range of American companies
and employees about the virtues of both employee ownership and social
market values.

The political genius of social market innovations is that they are attractive to liberals, because they promote equality and justice, as well as
to conservatives, because they do not require massive government inter-
vention and do offer ordinary citizens a greater stake in the marketplace.

In the 1970s, Senator Russell Long, a conservative Democrat from Louisiana, was the prime sponsor in the Senate for employee-ownership legislation, and the idea found considerable support in the Reagan White House as a strategy for building "people's capitalism." Liberal activists in universities, unions, and local communities also fight for employee ownership as a way to save jobs and increase workers' control.

Any idea that can draw such enthusiastic support from both sides of the political spectrum has the potential to be instituted on a large scale. At the same time, however, most of the more radical social market innovations have been resisted by powerful forces, as in the case of banks systematically denying credit to cooperatives. Mainstream businesses and politicians have also worked to water down innovations such as ESOPs to keep them from turning actual decision-making power over to workers. Nonetheless, those who seek real solutions to America's wilding crisis should hone the idea of the social market as a new public philosophy and the basis of a new legislative agenda.

Although government is not the prime mover in this emerging social market, it has helped midwife the new system and will have to play a much greater role if a new market order is to grow and preserve civil society. Government has to set up the legislative framework for corporate social charters, ESOPs, and worker cooperatives; establish the legal safeguards and guidelines for social investment of pension funds; provide encouragement through loans and tax credits for employee ownership and community-development funds; and help oversee and underwrite the entire new economic nexus. Its regulatory role will remain powerful for many years and will never disappear, for many public interests can be guaranteed only by the state. The government will not give marching orders to business or own the means of production as it does under communism or socialism; the social market is still a market system, infused with sensibilities of community.

There is special urgency now regarding children. One of every five American children lives in poverty, and public policy threatens to guarantee that the next generation will mature into uninhibited wilders. As civil society unravels, children are the most vulnerable group, being totally dependent on the love, moral guidance, and social spending that are casualties of the wilding culture. The state cannot raise and socialize children, but one of its highest priorities should be to help finance and save the institutions, including the family and schools, that can do the job. These are now in such desperate condition that further benign neglect is unacceptable; moreover, sensible and economical family and educational strategies have already been articulated by numerous national commissions and children's advocates such as the Children's Defense Fund. No antipoverty social market programs are utopian, and none need to be budget-busters.

The rise of the embryonic social market is part of a second American revolution, this one to ensure economic rights and to save the society liberated by the Revolution more than 200 years ago. Then, the issue was inventing a political constitution; now it involves rewriting the economic constitution. As in the first revolution, ordinary citizens will have to struggle against powerful, entrenched forces, the King Georges of contemporary America who are more dedicated to their own privileges than to saving civil society in America.

A New Bill of Rights?
The Politics of Civil Society

America's romance with individualism and the free market has its virtues, but it has clouded Americans' understanding of what makes society tick. Civil society arises only when individuals develop strong obligations to the larger "us" that can override the perennial, very human preoccupation with the self. Such larger commitments bloom only under special conditions: when the community shows that it cares so deeply for each of its members that each member fully understands his or her debt to society and seeks to pay it back in full.

The Japanese and Europeans, in their very different ways, seem to appreciate this deal, or contract, that preserves civil society. Japanese corporations have historically smothered the Japanese worker in a cocoon of secure employment, health benefits, housing, and other social necessities that make it almost impossible for most workers to imagine life outside of the group. Through their expansive welfare states, the Europeans deliver their own bushel of benefits and entitlements that citizens recognize as indispensable to personal survival and happiness. Both systems possess their own serious problems and are partially eroding in the face of global economic pressures, but they continue to succeed in creating an allegiance to the larger community that breeds immunity to the wilding epidemic.

Each civil society has to find its own way of inspiring its members' devotion, but all must deliver those rock-bottom necessities essential to the pursuit of life, liberty, and happiness. These include some level of personal safety, food, shelter, and a livelihood. Social orphans deprived of these essentials are unable to fulfill any larger obligation to society, for their existence is entirely consumed by the brutish struggle for personal survival.

The concept of such social necessities leads to the idea of social citizenship, an extension of the familiar but narrower notion of political citizenship. The rights to health care, housing, and a job can be seen as social rights, parallel to our political rights to the franchise and to free speech enshrined in our Constitution. Political rights apply to all citizens automatically, because they are the precondition of democracy as a system. Similarly, social rights should be extended automatically to everyone, for they are the precondition of civil society's survival.

The Japanese deliver such social rights through a paternalistic, corporate, largely private extended family, whereas the Europeans do it through the welfare state. America will have to find its own way. Ideally, the emerging institutions of the social market will eventually provide a local, democratic, and nonstatist solution. One possibility is an American version of the success achieved by Mondragon, a remarkable complex of more than 100 industrial cooperatives in the Basque region of Spain. Over the past 40 years, Mondragon has succeeded in guaranteeing job security, housing, health care, and education to its members, with scarcely any help from the state. Workers have created cooperative schools, hospitals, insurance companies, and banks that offer robust social security from birth to death. The Mondragon complex, which is the largest manufacturer of durable goods in Spain and employs thousands of worker-owners, has never permanently laid off a worker, reproducing the equivalent of the Japanese system of lifetime employment, while also inventing new cooperatives in one of the most impressive programs of job creation in the world.

Whether an American social market could evolve in such a direction is purely speculative, but clearly there are ways to provide social rights that are realistic, democratic, and do not require big and overly intrusive government. America is the only major industrialized country not to offer health care as a social right to all its citizens. In Germany and other European countries, the federal government is involved in collecting taxes to support national health care, but allows provincial councils and local communities to administer their own programs.

Although government is not the preferred agent in our society, it has a leading role to play in areas such as education, health care, and social welfare, where human need rather than profit is the only acceptable moral compass. Government is also the guarantor of last resort. When people are homeless, starving, or jobless, civil society has failed, and a wilding virus is activated. Remedies to these problems are not silly idealism or bleeding-heart liberalism, but a conservative and prudent defense of the social order that requires public action.

For this reason, legal scholars such as Columbia University law professor Louis Henkin are pointing to "genetic defects" in our Bill of Rights that constitutionally guarantee political but not social citizenship rights. Chief Justice William Rehnquist, in a 1989 Supreme Court decision, argued that the Constitution confers "no affirmative right to governmental aid, even when such aid may be necessary to secure life." This leads constitutional attorney Paul Savoy, former dean of the John F. Kennedy University School of Law, to point out that "our civil rights and civil liberties are rights in the negative sense" and "do not include affirmative obligations on government. We do not have a constitutional right to have the state provide us with health care, or give us shelter if we are homeless, or prevent a child from being beaten or from starving to death." A coalition of unions, environmentalists, and community groups have responded by calling for a second Bill of Rights that would entitle all citizens to the elementary social rights of shelter, food, and health care.[14]

Such social rights have already been embraced by most nations of the world and by the United Nations. The 1948 U.N. Universal Declaration of Human Rights explicitly embraces the right of all people to employment, shelter, education, and health care. The International Labor Organization, a U.N. agency, spells out the rights of all workers to associate freely in unions of their choice and to earn a living wage. There are also U.N. agreements on the rights of women, children, and the environment. Unfortunately, many of these rights are not enforced—and the U.N. has no mechanism to do so. To combat wilding in the global economy, it is essential that the U.S. government, a signatory of many of the U.N. human rights documents, move aggressively to support international means of enforcing social rights both abroad and at home.[15]

Social rights are not a free ride for the population, for with them come demanding social obligations. Citizenship is an intimate dance of rights and obligations, and social citizens will need to enthusiastically embrace the moral obligations that come with their new entitlements. This means not only willingly paying the taxes required to keep civil society healthy, but also devoting time and effort to community-building at work, in the neighborhood, and in the country at large.

The problem with the Left is that it demands rights without spelling out the obligations that have to accompany them; the problem with the Right is that it expects obligations to be fulfilled without ceding social rights in return. Both positions are absurd because rights and obligations are flip sides of civil society's coin of the realm. We need a new politic that marries the Left's moral passion for rights with the Right's sober recognition of duty.

Defending Our Lives:
Getting from Here to There

But what do we do now? Americans are a pragmatic people who want down-to-earth answers. Although there is no recipe or magic formula, we can act now to stop the wilding epidemic. If we want to survive with our humanity intact, we have no alternative.

Since wilding can destroy society, we are all fighting to stay alive. Obviously, if we each felt we had a desperate illness, we would mobilize ourselves to act immediately to save ourselves. But since wilding is a societal crisis, not a biological illness, individuals can feel a deceptive immunity. It is possible to feel healthy, have fun, and enjoy life as society begins to come undone.

But as the epidemic spreads, everyone will increasingly feel at risk. The personal meaning of the wilding crisis is that we each have to spend more and more time simply defending our lives, defending our property, defending our livelihood, defending our health, defending our physical safety, defending our egos. This imposes a terrible burden on the individual, and it can easily fuel the "me" mentality at the heart of the problem, but it also unlocks the riddle of what to do. Not only will the illusion of immunity diminish, but the wisdom of dealing with the underlying disease, not just the symptoms, will become more apparent.

One can start defending one's life, as Albert Brooks's 1990s film comedy of that title suggests, either wisely or foolishly. The shortsighted approach involves trying to save oneself by abandoning everyone else, like the suburbanites who cocoon themselves within homes wired with the latest security technology and who refuse to pay taxes to support the center city. Robert Reich suggests that such a "politics of secession" is sweeping upper-middle-class America.[16] If so, it is a blind and morally unsustainable choice, for it creates short-term symptomatic relief while worsening the disease.

Because the disease is social, so too must be the cure. As the social infrastructure begins to ulcerate and bleed, the rational long-term way to defend one's life is to help repair the damaged societal tissue, whether it be potholes in the road, hungry people sleeping on grates, or sociopathic competitiveness at the office. Doing the right thing, then, is defending one's life by cooperating to build up community strength and bolster personal and collective resistance. This requires no saintly sacrifice for the common good, but rather a tough-minded and clear-eyed assessment of where the threat lies. When facing a wilding threat, the first question to ask is, "What in my social environment or me is creating this threat?" Once that question is answered, the next one is, "What can I do about it?" Some cases of wilding will require purely personal change: falling back on all one's psychological and moral strength, as well as love and support from family, friends, or mentors, to counter wilding impulses within oneself or susceptibility to wilding influence in the environment. Most cases will also require acting for some form of social change to extirpate the external poison, whether at work, in the neighborhood, or in the White House; this is typically achievable only with the help of others.

Fortunately, the wisdom of social action is obvious in a huge variety of circumstances, and Americans are already responding, especially where their own health is involved. When kids in Woburn, Massachusetts, were getting sick because of toxic chemicals, parents got together to clean up the toxic dump and hold the wilding factory accountable. Americans are recognizing that staying healthy has become a political action project requiring a massive environmental cleanup, and they are not waiting for lackadaisical governments to take the lead. "People are recognizing they can in fact control their environment," Hal Hiemstra, a Washington environmental activist notes. "They're starting to say, 'we've had it.'" The *Boston Globe* reports that "an environmental wake-up call [is] being sounded nationwide by communities alarmed by the federal government's inertia and inspired by their own sense of power to reshape the landscape." These activists are not only defending their lives but, the *Globe* observes, "are local heroes on planetary matters."[17]

Heroes of a different sort are the residents of suburban communities around Minneapolis, who swam against the tide and rejected the politics of secession, the suburban wilding that helped push Bridgeport, Connecticut, into Chapter Eleven bankruptcy and left New York City and hundreds of other cities teetering on the brink. The Minnesota suburbs joined with Minneapolis to form a regional pact "whereby any community enjoying 40 percent more than the average growth of the region in any given year would have to share with the other signers of the pact." Such apparent sacrifice for the larger good is just plain common sense, because if the city center failed, it would bring the surrounding communities down with it. The great irony, as John Shannon of the Urban Institute notes, "is that Minneapolis is now enjoying boom times and must pay out to the suburbs." A modern Aesop's fable, it shows how cooperation for the common good is, indeed, a form of enlightened self-interest.[18]

We can begin to cure the wilding sickness by doing more of what we have always done well and doing it better: taking responsibility for our lives through civic participation. Tocqueville was amazed at the richness of America's democracy; its dense web of voluntary associations and democratic town meetings made it unique. "The free institutions which the inhabitants of the United States possess, and the political rights of which they make so much use," Tocqueville explained, "remind every citizen, and in a thousand ways, that he lives in society." In other words, democracy, and more democracy, is the best antidote for wilding and the most nourishing food for the social infrastructure.[19]

Americans have become apathetic and indifferent to national politics, but we still retain our propensity to join together in what Tocqueville called "an immense assemblage of associations." One researcher suggests that there are now more than 500,000 self-help groups in the United States, with more than 15 million members; many, whether alcoholics, abused children, battered spouses, or codependents, are casualties of the wilding epidemic who, by joining with others, are taking enlightened first steps toward not only recovering personally but also rebuilding civil society. The same can be said of the millions of others involved in volunteer efforts and political activism at local or higher levels.[20]

Millions of Americans recognize that giving back can be both fun and morally compelling, and they are serving their communities in movements to help the homeless, feed the hungry, care for AIDS patients, tutor the illiterate, protect the environment, and help organize America's workers and poor people. Many recognize that in addition to individual volunteers, we need sustained social movements that can provide the voice and muscle for ordinary citizens against the power of giant, greedy corporations and unresponsive government. This will require, most of all, the resurrection of a labor movement that speaks for social justice and economic democracy.

On my own campus, many students who have engaged in community service work have begun to realize that service is not enough. While it helps individuals in trouble, it does not solve the societal problems that put people in difficulty in the first place. Students who work in soup kitchens begin to ask why there are so many hungry people, and those working in battered women's shelters ask why there is so much domestic violence. This leads them to recognize that it will take collective action, that is, social movements aimed at changing institutions, to truly solve the underlying causes of the problems that plague the people they want to help.

Anti-sweatshop activists on campus have joined forces with the labor movement to end corporate wilding here and around the world. The labor movement, while demonized by many U.S. business leaders, is becoming a genuine voice for the community at large. Recall that "solidarity forever" has always been the rallying cry of the labor movement and that as corporations threaten community at home and abroad, the very concept of "union" tells us what we need: people coming together to defend human values against greed and exploitation.

Other social movements are also vital for people seeking to end the wilding crisis. I discussed in Chapter 4 the post-Seattle global justice movement that is bringing together students, workers, environmentalists, feminists, and civil rights groups from around the world to forge a new world community based on human rights rather than money. Each of these movements has its own agenda essential to combating aspects of the wilding crisis; as they learn to work together for justice at home and abroad, they offer the best chance to make a difference that we have seen in a long time. Anyone concerned with the wilding crisis should learn about these different movements and join them. For in these movements lies the chance not only of changing the world but of creating a new form of community for oneself.

Americans' indifference to national politics reflects less pure selfishness or apathy than despair about leaders and the absence of real choices. America desperately needs a new generation of political leaders who will tell the truth about the wilding crisis and articulate a new moral vision. But because no such leaders are now in view, the burden falls on the rest of us, where it ultimately belongs.

Notes

Chapter 1

1. APBNews.com, 2000. "Central Park Groping Victims Rise to 24." APB News.com, June 14, pp. 1–2. Retrieved from APBNews.com on June 14, 2000; ABCnews.com. 2000. "New Reward in Park Attacks." ABCnews.com. Retrieved from http://abcnews.go.com/sections/us/DailyNews/central park000617.html on June 18, 2000; Cloud, John. 2001. "The Bad Sunday in the Park." Time.com. Retrieved from Time.com on February 7, 2001.
2. APBnews, 2000.
3. Cloud, 2001.
4. "Move to Kill Victim Described by Defendant in Jogger Rape." 1989. *New York Times*, November 2, p. 1.
5. "Testimony Has Youths Joyous After Assault." 1989. *New York Times*, November 4, p. 1.
6. "Three Youths Jailed in Rape of Jogger." 1990. *Boston Globe*, September 12, p. 9.
7. "The Central Park Rape Sparks a War of Words." 1989. *Newsweek*, May 15, p. 40.
8. Williams, Patricia J. 2002. "Reasons for Doubt." *The Nation*, December 30, p. 10.
9. Ibid.
10. Graham, Renee. 1990. "Hoax Seen Playing on Fear, Racism." *Boston Globe*, January 11, p. 24.
11. Graham, Renee. 1990. "Fur Store, Quiet Street Are Now Macabre Meccas." *Boston Globe*, January 16, p. 20.
12. Turnbull, Colin. 1987. *The Mountain People*. New York: Simon Schuster.
13. Ibid., p. 86.
14. Ibid., p. 153.
15. Ibid., Back cover.
16. Ibid., p. 132.
17. Ibid., p. 132.
18. Ibid., p. 137.
19. I am indebted to Mike Miller for suggesting the terms "instrumental" and "expressive" wilding.

20. I am indebted to Mike Miller for his suggestion of "two Americas."

21. For an excellent book on the subject see: Taylor, John. 1989. *Circus of Ambition: The Culture of Wealth and Power in the Eighties*. New York: Warner Books.

22. Trump, Donald, with Tony Schwartz. 1987. *Trump: The Art of the Deal*. New York: Warner Books.

23. Lewis, Michael. 2001. "Jonathen Lebed's Extracurricular Activities." *New York Times Magazine,* February 25, pp. 26ff.

24. Callahan, David. 2001. "Here's to Bad Times." *New York Times,* February 5, p. A21.

25. Taylor, *Circus of Ambition,* p. 8.

26. Shames, Laurence. 1989. *The Hunger for More: Searching for Values in an Age of Greed*. New York: Times Books.

27. Ibid., p. 27.

28. Reich, Robert B. 1991. "Secession of the Successful." *New York Times Magazine,* January 20, pp. 16–17, 42–45.

29. De Tocqueville, Alexis. 1985. *Democracy in America*. Vol. II. New York: Knopf (originally published 1840), pp. 137–138.

30. Durkheim, cited in Lukes, Steven. 1973. *Emile Durkheim: His Life and Work, a Historical and Critical Study*. New York: Penguin, p. 207.

31. Ibid.

32. Ibid.

33. Marx, Karl, cited in Tucker, Robert C. 1972. *The Marx-Engels Reader*. New York: Norton, p. 337.

34. Lukes, *Emile Durkheim,* p. 218.

Chapter 2

1. "Wife of Slain NFL Player Indicted for Murder." October 17, 2000. Retrieved from http://cnews.tribune.com/news/story/0,1162, wbdc-sports-68648,00.html on 2/2001.

2. "East Texas Pharmacist Pleads Guilty to Wife's Murder." March 11, 1998. Retrieved from http://www.reporternews.com/texas/murd0311.html on 2/2001.

3. McGinniss, Joe. 1989. *Blind Faith*. New York: Signet, p. 420.

4. Ibid., p. 62.

5. Ibid., p. 86.

6. Ibid., p. 89.

7. Ibid., p. 87.

8. Ibid., p. 308.

9. Ibid., p. 414.

10. Ibid., p. 297.

11. Ibid., p. 436.

12. Bass, Alison. 1990. "Cold-Blooded Killers Rarely Stand Out from the Crowd." *Boston Globe,* January 15, p. 34.
13. Ibid.
14. Fox, James Alan, and Jack Levin. 1990. "Inside the Mind of Charles Stuart." *Boston Magazine,* April, pp. 66ff.
15. Bass, "Cold-Blooded Killers," p. 34.
16. Fox and Levin, "Inside the Mind of Charles Stuart."
17. Hamil, Pete. 1990. "Murder on Mulholland." *Esquire,* June, pp. 67–71.
18. Hughes, Kathleen, and David Jefferson. 1990. "Why Would Brothers Who Had Everything Murder Their Parents?" *Wall Street Journal,* March 20, p. A1.
19. "A Beverly Hills Paradise Lost." *Time,* March 26, 1990, pp. 64ff.
20. Ibid.
21. Ibid., p. 69.
22. Hughes and Jefferson, "Why Would Brothers?" p. A10.
23. "A Beverly Hills Paradise," p. 69.
24. Ibid., p. 72; Hughes and Jefferson, "Why Would Brothers?" p. 1.
25. Hughes and Jefferson, "Why Would Brothers?"
26. "A Beverly Hills Paradise," p. 69.
27. Hughes and Jefferson, "Why Would Brothers?" p. 1.
28. Hussman, Lawrence. 1983. *Dreiser and His Fiction.* Philadelphia: University of Pennsylvania Press.
29. Sennott, Charles M. 1994. "Kin Have Misgivings about Death Penalty." *Boston Globe,* November 8, p. 10.
30. Adler, Jerry. 1994. "Innocents Lost," *Newsweek,* November 14, pp. 27ff. See also "Night That Turned Mom into a Killer." 1994. *National Enquirer,* November 14, pp. 28ff.
31. Sennott, Charles M. 1994. "Bid to Climb Social Ladder Seen in Smith's Fall to Despair." *Boston Globe,* November 8, pp. 1, 10.

Chapter 3

1. Barstow, David, and Sarah Kershaw. 2000. "Teenagers Accused of Killing for a Free Meal." *New York Times,* September 7, p. 1; Reeves, Jay. 2000. "Woman Given 13-Year Prison Term in 'Road Rage' Slaying." *Boston Globe,* December 5, p. A6.
2. Bach, Elizabeth. 2003. "Police Say 'Road Rage' Driver Struck Officer with Car." *Boston Globe,* June 25, p. B1.
3. Trausch, Susan. 1990. "The Generous Greed Machine." *Boston Globe,* March 4, p. 14.
4. Polner, Rob. "A Real Education in the New York City School System." *In These Times,* April 11–17, p. 12.
5. Sloan, Allan. 1996. "Jobs—The Hit Men." *Newsweek,* February 26.

6. Kaplan, Don. 2001. "Host: Rich Wouldn't Survive New Cast." *New York Post*, January 11. Retrieved from www.foxnews.com/entertainment/011101/survivor_hatch.sml on 2/2001.

7. Sepinwall, Alan. 2001. "Extreme TV: The (Rear) End of Civilization as We Know It." Newhouse News Service, February 2. Retrieved from http://www0.mercurycenter.com/tv/center/extremetv.htm on 2/2001.

8. Collins, Chuck, and Felice Yeskel. 2000. *Economic Apartheid in America*. New York: New Press.

9. Derber, Charles. 2000. *Corporation Nation*. New York: St. Martin's Press.

10. "Warning: The Standard of Living Is Slipping." 1987. *Business Week*, April 20, p. 48.

11. Phillips, Kevin. 1990. *Politics of the Rich and Poor*. New York: Random House, p. 10.

12. "Warning," pp. 46, 52; "The Face of the Recession." 1990. *Boston Globe*, August 14, pp. 24–25.

13. "Warning," pp. 46, 52.

14. Kanter, Donald, and Philip Mirvis. 1989. *The Cynical Americans*. San Francisco: Jossey-Bass, pp. 10, 291.

15. Fiske, Edward B. 1990. "Fabric of Campus Life Is in Tatters, a Study Says." *New York Times*, April 30, p. A15.

16. Knox, Richard A. 1994. "Binge Drinking Linked to Campus Difficulties." *Boston Globe*, December 7, pp. 1, 15.

17. Walsh, Pamela. 1995. "Second Harvard Student Pleads Guilty to Stealing." *Boston Globe*, February 24, p. 8; "Florida Law Student Held in a Murder Plot." 1995. *New York Times*, February 24, p. A16; Johnston, David. 2001. "Second Killing in a Year," *New York Times*, February 5, p. A11.

18. Fiske, "Fabric of Campus Life," p. A15.

19. Butterfield, Fox. 1991. "Scandal over Cheating at M.I.T. Stirs Debate on Limits of Teamwork." *New York Times*, May 22, p. 12.

20. "College Admission Offices Targeting Fraudulent Essays." 2000. *Boston Globe*, November 27, pp. 1, B4.

21. Flint, Anthony. 1992. "Student Markets Primer on the Art of Cheating." *Boston Globe*, February 3, pp. 1, 13.

22. Celis, William, III. 1991. "Blame to Share in Overcharging of U.S. for Research." *New York Times*, May 12, p. 1.

23. Kowalczyk, Liz. 2001. "New Steps Urged on University Research Bias." *Boston Globe*, February 20, pp. A1, D6.

24. Bourgois, Philippe. 1989. "Just Another Night on Crack Street." *New York Times Magazine*, November 12, pp. 53ff.

25. Ibid., p. 62.

26. Ibid., p. 64.

27. Ibid., p. 62.

28. Ibid., p. 65.
29. Ibid., p. 94.
30. Ibid., p. 94.
31. Adler, William. 1995. *Land of Opportunity: One Family's Quest for the American Dream in the Age of Crack.* Boston: Atlantic Monthly Press.
32. Ibid. See also Frankel, Max. 1995. "Drug War, II." *New York Times Magazine*, January 29.

Chapter 4

1. "Made in the USA?" 2001. National Labor Committee, New York, February 12. Retrieved from www.nlcnet.org on February 12, 2001.
2. Herbert, Bob. 1994. "Terror in Toyland." *New York Times,* December 21, p. A27.
3. Anderson, Sarah, John Cavanaugh, and Thea Lee. 2000. *Field Guide to the Global Economy.* New York: The New Press.
4. For a concise, readable interpretation of globalization as a "race to the bottom," see Brecher, Jeremy and Tim Costello. 1998. *Global Village or Global Pillage?* 2d ed. Boston: South End Press.
5. Kernaghan, Charles. 2000. "Made in China: Behind the Label." New York: National Labor Committee.
6. Brown, Sherrod. 2001. "Pentagon Sweatshops." *The Progressive,* February, pp. 31–32.
7. Barnet, Richard, and John Cavanaugh. 1994. *Global Dreams.* New York: Simon & Schuster, pp. 321ff. See also Fuentes, Annette and Barbara Ehrenreich. 1992. *Women in the Global Factory.* Boston: South End Press, pp. 10ff.
8. La Botz, Dan. 1992. *Mask of Democracy: Labor Suppression in Mexico Today.* Boston: South End Press, p. 162.
9. International Labor Rights Fund. 2001. "Report to Universities Regarding the Kukdong International Conflict in Axtlico, Puebla, Mexico" Report on Internet, January 25. Worker Rights Consortium. 2001. Letter to Nike, Scott Nova (WRC Executive Director), January 14.
10. Dillon, Sam. 2001. "Profits Raise Pressure on Border Factories." *New York Times,* February 15, pp. A1, A9.
11. La Botz, *Mask of Democracy,* p. 164.
12. Ibid., pp. 164–68.
13. Thompson, Ginger. 2001. "Chasing Mexico's Dream into Squalor." *New York Times,* February 11, pp. A1, A8.
14. Ibid.
15. See Derber, Charles. 2003. *People Before Profit.* New York: Picador, for a discussion of the new movements and their vision of a just global economy.

16. Barnet and Cavanaugh, *Global Dreams*. See also Phillips, Kevin. 1994. *Arrogant Capital*. Boston: Little, Brown, chap. 1.

17. Brecher and Costello, *Global Village or Global Pillage?*

18. Derber, Charles. 2000. *Corporation Nation*. New York: St. Martin's Press, chap. 14; Brecher, Jeremy, Tim Costello, and Brendan Smith. 2000. *Globalization from Below*. Boston: South End Press.

19. Brecher and Costello, *Global Village or Global Pillage?*

20. Derber, *Corporation Nation*.

21. Ibid.

Chapter 5

1. Behr, Peter, and April Witt. 2002. "Visionary's Dream Led to Risky Business." *Washington Post,* July 28, p. A1.

2. Raghavan, Anita, Kathryn Kranhold, and Alexei Barrionuevo. 2002. "How Enron Bosses Created a Culture of Pushing Limits." *Wall Street Journal,* August 26. Retrieved August 26, 2002.

3. Nocera, Joseph, Jeremy Kahn, David Rynecki, Clifton Leaf, et al. 2002. "System Failure." *Fortune Magazine,* June 24.

4. Associated Press. 2002. "Andersen Auditor Cuts Plea Deal." *CBS News.com,* April 9. Retrieved April 9, 2002.

5. Tran, Mark. 2002. "Arthur Andersen Appeals for Sympathy." *The Guardian,* January 29. Retrieved January 29, 2002.

6. Goldstein, Matthew. 2003. "Four Merrill Bankers Charged in Enron Scandal," *The Street.com,* March 17. Retrieved March 17, 2003.

7. Kurt Eichenwald with Riva D. Atlas. 2003. "Two Banks Settle Accusations They Aided in Enron Fraud." *New York Times,* July 29, 2003, p. 1; Goldstein, Matthew. 2003. "Merrill's Latest Fine Is Tip of the Iceberg." *The Street.com,* February 21. Retrieved February 21, 2003.

8. Teather, David. 2002. "The Whores of Wall Street," *The Guardian,* October 2. Retrieved October 2, 2002.

9. Goldstein, Matthew. 2003. "Enron Examiner Plans 1,500-Page Valentine," *The Street.com,* January 17. Retrieved January 17, 2003.

10. Iwata, Edward. 2002. "Merrill Lynch Probe Widens," *USA Today.* July 31, p. B2. Retrieved July 31, 2002.

11. PBS Online and WGBH/Frontline. 2002. "Who Dropped the Ball," *Frontline.* Retrieved from www.pbsonline.com on July 20, 2002. See also PBS Online and WGBH/Frontline, 2002. "Dot Con," *Frontline.* Retrieved from www.pbsonline.com on January 24, 2002.

12. Morgensen, Gretchen. 2002. "Analyst Coached WorldCom Chief on His Script," *New York Times,* February 27, p. A1.

13. Labaton, Stephen. 2003. "Wall Street Settlement: The Overview; 10 Wall St. Firms Reach Settlement in Analyst Inquiry." *New York Times,* April 29, p. A1.

14. Nocera, Joseph, et al. "System Failure."

15. See Derber, Charles. 2003. *People before Profit.* New York: St. Martin's Press. See also Derber, Charles. 2000. *Corporation Nation.* New York: St. Martin's Press.

16. Center for Responsive Politics. 2002. "Enron's Contributions to Federal Candidates and Parties, 1989–2001." Retrieved from www. opensecrets. org/laterts/u6/enron-totals.asp on June 16, 2003.

17. Heller, Doug. 2001. "Commentary; Enron Gets Zapped by its Own Greed," *Los Angeles Times,* November 30, p. B15. Retrieved November 30, 2001.

18. Nocera, Joseph, et al. "System Failure."

Chapter 6

1. I want to thank my colleague, Michael Malec, for sharing some of his own very valuable insights about the issues addressed in this chapter. Virtually all the documentation I rely on in this chapter comes from the remarkable reporting by the *Boston Globe* Spotlight team. The journalists have compiled their reporting into a book, *Betrayal: The Crisis in the Catholic Church* (Boston: Little Brown and Co., 2002). I have referenced this chapter from specific articles largely reported in the *Boston Globe.* For the Geoghan story, see Rezendes, Michael, et al. 2002. "Church Allowed Abuse by Priest for Years." *Boston Globe,* January 6. Retrieved January 6, 2002 from http://www.boston.com/globe/spotlight/abuse/stories/010602_geoghan.htm.

2. Rezendes et al. 2002. "Church Allowed Abuse," p. 3.

3. Andersen, Ken. N.D. "Paul Shanley." *Ken Anderson—A Texas Paramedic in Maine: Overview of Bible History.* Retrieved from http://www. kenanderson.net/bible/paul_shanley.html.

4. Rezendes, Michael and Matt Carroll. 2002. "Boston Diocese Gave Letter of Assurance about Shanley," *Boston Globe,* April 8, 2002. Retrieved from http://www.boston.com/globe/spotlight/abuse/stories/040802_shanley.htm on April 8, 2002 .

5. Farragher, Thomas. 2002. "Admission of Awareness Damning for Law." *Boston Globe,* December 14, p. A15. Retrieved from http://www.boston. com/globe/spotlight/abuse/stories3/121402_admission.htm on December 14, 2002.

6. Robinson, Walter and Matt Carroll. 2002. "Documents Show Church Long Supported Geoghan." *Boston Globe,* January 24, pp. 3–4. Retrieved from http://www.boston.com/globe/spotlight/abuse/stories/012402_documents.htm on January 24, 2002.

7. Robinson and Carroll. 2002. "Documents Show Church."

8. Rezendes and Carroll. 2002. "Boston Diocese Gave Letter," pp. 1–2.

9. Robinson, Walter V. 2002. "Judge Finds Records, Law at Odds." *Boston Globe,* November 26, p. A1. Retrieved from http://www.boston.com/globe/spotlight/abuse/stories3/112602_records.htm on November 26, 2002. Robinson, Walter V., and Michael Rezendes. 2003. "Abuse scandal far deeper than disclosed," *Boston Globe,* July 24, p. 1.

10. Belkin, Douglas. 2003. "Priest Castigates Springfield Diocese for Abuse Dealings." *Boston Globe,* February 17, p. B1.

11. Ibid., p. B1.

12. Ibid., p. B7.

13. Ibid.

14. Ibid.

15. Learn about Voice of the Faithful by going to its website at http://www.votf.org.

16. Voice of the Faithful. 2002. "Structural Change Working Group Report as of 9/26/02." Cited at http://www.votf.org/Structural_Change/structural.html, pp. 1–3.

17. For information on ARCC, e-mail arccangel@charter.net. I want to thank Michael Malec for informing me of ARCC and providing me with some of its documents.

18. Association for the Rights of Catholics in the Church (ARCC). N.D. "Charter of the Rights of Catholics in the Church, Fifth Edition." Retrieved from http://arcc-catholic-rights.org/charter.htm.

19. ARCC, N.D.

20. ARCC, N.D. See Appendix 1: Relevant Canons from the Revised Code of Canon Law, pp. 1–2.

Chapter 7

1. "Boy Accused of Needle Attack." 2001. *New York Times,* February 2, p. A2.

2. Wolf, Craig. 1989. "Ten Teen-Age Girls Held in Upper Broadway Pinprick Attacks." *New York Times,* November 4, p. 27.

3. Stepp, Laura. 2000. "U.S. Survey Focuses on At-Risk Teens." 2000. *Boston Globe*, November 30, p. A4.

4. "First Grader Shot Dead at School." February 29, 2000. Retrieved from http://abcnews.go.com/sections/us/DailyNews/shooting000229.html on February 29, 2001.

5. "Violence in U. S. Schools." 2000. Retrieved from http://abcnews.go.com/sections/us/DailyNews/schoolshootings990420.html in February 2001.

6. "Fears Rise of a City Consumed by Violence." 1990. *Boston Globe*, March 15, p. 12.

7. Ibid.; Jacobs, Sally. 1990. "As Streets Turn Deadly, Youths Revise Their Survival Code." *Boston Globe,* February 24, p. 1.

8. Vaishnav, Anand. 2001. "Perception and Reality in Boston's Safe Schools." *Boston Globe,* February 18, p. D3; Tippit, Sarah. 2001. "Poll Says Violence Is Common in Schools." *Boston Globe,* April 2, p. A-8.

9. Ashbrook, Tom. 1989. "A View from the East," *Boston Globe Sunday Magazine,* February 19, p. 71.

10. Ibid., pp. 71–72.

11. Ibid., p. 76.

12. Mitchell, Philip. 1990. "Saving State Roads." *Boston Globe,* March, p. 11; "Aging Roads, Bridges, Get Scant Notice." 1990. *Boston Globe,* April 11, p. 20.

13. Albert, Michael. 1990. "At the Breaking Point?" *Z Magazine,* May, p. 17; DeMarco, Susan and Jim Hightower. 1988. "You've Got to Spread It Around." *Mother Jones,* May, p. 36; Sege, Irene. 1990. "Poverty, Disease, Poor Education Imperil Nation's Youth, Panel Says." *Boston Globe,* April 27, p. 6.

14. Honan, William. 1995. "14 Million Pupils in Unsuitable or Unsafe Schools, Report Says." *New York Times,* February 1, p. A21.

15. "Consensus Fuels Ascent of Europe." 1990. *Boston Globe,* May 13, p. 19.

16. Kelly, Michael. 1995. "Rip It Up." *New Yorker,* January 23, pp. 32–39.

17. Derber, Charles. 1993. "Bush's Other War." *Tikkon,* summary.

18. Mitchell, Alison. 2001. "Moderate Republicans Oppose Bush Tax Plan as Democrats Offer Their Own." *New York Times,* February 16, p. A13.

19. "Bush Tax Plan Sent to Congress." 2001. *New York Times,* February 9, pp. A1, A14.

20. Johnston, David Cay. 2001. "Dozens of Rich Americans Join in Fight to Retain the Estate Tax." *New York Times,* February 14, pp. A1, A18.

21. "A Bad Break." 2001. *Boston Globe,* editorial, February 16.

22. Lancelot, Jill, and Ralph de Genero. 1995. "Green Scissors Snip $33 Billion." *New York Times,* January 31, p. A21.

23. Kuttner, Robert. 1980. *Revolt of the Haves.* New York: Simon & Schuster, p. 10.

24. Powers, John. 1990. "Whatever Happened to the Common Good?" *Boston Globe Magazine,* April 1, pp. 16–17, 38–42.

25. Gordon, Suzanne. 1990. "Our Town Crumbles as Residents Idly Sit By." *Boston Globe,* February 24, pp. A1, A22.

26. These interviews were skillfully carried out by Boston College graduate students David Croteau and Mary Murphy.

27. Ross, Jeffery Ian, ed. 2000. *Controlling State Crime.* New Brunswick, NJ: Transaction Press.

28. Barsamian, David. 2001. "Angela Davis." *The Progressive,* February, pp. 33–38.

29. Ibid.

30. Mauer, Marc, and Tracy Huling. 1995. "Young Black Americans and the Criminal Justice System: Five Years Later." Internet published (www.sentencingproject.org): The Sentencing Project.
31. Barsamian, "Angela Davis."
32. Jackson, Derrick. 2001. "Superfly Scores in Harlem." *Boston Globe,* February 16, p. A19.
33. Ibid.
34. Bugliosi, Vincent. 2001. "None Dare Call It Treason." *The Nation.* February 5, pp. 11–19.

Chapter 8

1. Wallerstein, Immanuel. 2000. *The Essential Wallerstein.* New York: The New Press.
2. Arrighi, Giovanni. 1994. *The Long Twentieth Century.* London: Verso.
3. MacFarquhar, Neil. 2002. "Humiliation and Rage Stalk the Arab World." *New York Times,* April 13, Section 4, p. 1.
4. Sachs, Susan. 2003. "Egyptian Intellectual Speaks of the Arab World's Despair." *New York Times,* April 8, pp. B1–2.
5. Shadid, Anthony. 2003. "Hospitals Overwhelmed by Living and the Dead." *Washington Post,* April 8, p. A29; Thanassis, Cambanis. 2003. "Iraqis in Basra Weigh Freedom's Cost," *Boston Globe,* April 8, p. B1.
6. Falk, Richard. 2002. "The New Bush Doctrine." *The Nation,* July 15. Retrieved from http://www.thenation.com/doc.mhtml?i=20020715&s=falk) on July 15, 2002.
7. *Los Angeles Times.* 2003. "Weapons of Mass Destruction May Not Be Found, Bush Says." *Boston Globe,* April 25, p. A17
8. Dean, John. 2003. "Is Lying about the Reason for a War an Impeachable Offense?" CNN.com, June 6. Retrieved from www.cnn.com/2003/LAW/06/06/findlaw.analysis.dean.wmd/index.html on June 6, 2003.
9. Kristof, Nicholas D. 2003. "White House in Denial." *New York Times,* June 13, p. A33.
10. Lemann, Nicholas. 2002. "The Next World Order." *The New Yorker,* April 1; Bacevich, Andrew J. 2002. *American Empire: The Realities and Consequences of U.S. Diplomacy.* Cambridge, MA: Harvard University Press, pp. 44–45.
11. See Lemann, "The Next World Order." See also Project for the New American Century. 2000. "Rebuilding America's Defense." Author: Washington, D.C.
12. See Henriques, Diana B. 2003. "Who Will Put Iraq Back Together?" *New York Times,* March 23, Section 3, p. 1
13. Bumiller, Elisabeth and Alison Mitchell. 2002. "Bush Aides See Political Pluses in Security Plan." *New York Times,* June 15, p. A1.

14. For a recent mainstream discussion of the economic foundations of U.S. military interventions, see Bacevich 2002, *American Empire.* For a more radical view emphasizing many of the same themes, see Chomsky, Noam. 1993. *What Uncle Sam Really Wants.* Tucson, AZ: Odonian Press.

Chapter 9

1. Wolfe, Alan. 1989. *Whose Keeper? Social Science and Moral Obligation.* Berkeley: University of California Press.
2. Tocqueville, Alexis de. [1840] 1985. *Democracy in America.* Vol. II. New York: Knopf, pp. 119–20, 121, 123.
3. Ibid., p. 128.
4. Ibid., p. 129.
5. Preer, Robert. 1991. "Volunteers Plug Cash Gap in the Suburbs." *Boston Globe,* June 9, pp. 1, 8.
6. Teltsch, Kathleen. 1991. "Nowadays, Robin Hood Gets the Rich to Give to the Poor." *New York Times,* June 3, p. B1.
7. Hodgkinson, Virginia Ann and Murray S. Weitzman. 1989. *Dimensions of the Independent Sector.* Washington, DC: Independent Sector, pp. 7–9.
8. Combs, James. 1984. *Polpop: Politics and Popular Culture in America.* Bowling Green, OH: Bowling Green University Popular Press, p. 29.
9. Ibid., p. 34.
10. Phillips, Kevin. 1990. *Politics of Rich and Poor.* New York: Random House, chap. 1.
11. "Consensus Fuels Ascent of Europe." 1990. *Boston Globe,* May 13, p. 19.
12. Bruyn, Severyn. 1991. *A Future for the American Economy.* Stanford, CA: Stanford University Press. See also Bruyn, Severyn. 1987. *The Field of Social Investment.* Cambridge: Cambridge University Press; Bruyn, Severyn, and James Meehan. 1985. *Beyond the Market and the State.* Philadelphia: Temple University Press; Lowry, Ritchie. 1991. *Good Money.* New York: W. W. Norton.
13. Bruyn, *A Future for the American Economy.*
14. Savoy, Paul. 1991. "Time for a Second Bill of Rights." *The Nation,* June 17, pp. 815–16.
15. Ibid.
16. Reich, Robert. 1992. *Work of Nations.* New York: Vintage.
17. Tye, Larry. 1991. "Local Heroes on Planetary Matters." *Boston Globe,* June 22, p. 3.
18. Loth, Renee. 1991. "Small Cities, Big Problems." *Boston Globe,* June 23, pp. A25, A28.
19. Tocqueville, *Democracy in America.*
20. Marx, Gary T. 1994. "Fragmentation and Cohesion in American Society." In R. Dynes and K. Tierney, *Disasters, Collective Behavior, and Social Organization,* Newark, DE: University of Delaware Press.

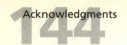
Grateful acknowledgment is made for permission to reprint the following:

James Alan Fox and Jack Levin, excerpts from "Inside the Mind of Charles Stuart," *Boston Magazine* (April 1990). Copyright © 1990 by Boston Magazine, Inc., a subsidiary of METROCORP. Reprinted with the permission of *Boston Magazine*.

Kathleen Hughes and David Jefferson, excerpts from "Why Would Brothers Who Had Everything Murder Their Parents?" *The Wall Street Journal* (March 20, 1990). Copyright © 1990 by Dow Jones & Company, Inc. Reprinted with the permission of *The Wall Street Journal*.

[Approximately 46 words from personal communication by Noam Chomsky with the author, 1991.] CREDIT: Reprinted with the permission of Noam Chomsky.

Connie Bruck, excerpts from *The Predator's Ball* (New York: Penguin, 1988). Copyright © 1988 by Connie Bruck. Reprinted with permission of Simon & Schuster, Inc., and Penguin Books USA.

Susan Trausch, excerpts from "The Generous Greed Machine," *Boston Globe* (March 4, 1990). Copyright © 1990 by the Globe Newspaper Company. Reprinted with the permission of *The Boston Globe*.

Rob Polner, excerpts from "A Real Education in the New York City School System," *In These Times* (April 11–17, 1990). Reprinted with the permission of *In These Times*, a biweekly news magazine published in Chicago.

Excerpt from "Warning: The Standard of Living Is Slipping," *Business Week* (April 20, 1987). Copyright © 1987 by McGraw-Hill, Inc. Reprinted with the permission of *Business Week*.

Phillipe Bourgois, Excerpts from *The New York Times* article. Reprinted with the permission of the author.

Craig Wolf, excerpts from "Ten Teen-Age Girls Held in Upper Broadway Pinprick Attacks," *The New York Times* (November 8, 1989). Copyright © 1989 by The New York Times Company. Reprinted with the permission of *The New York Times*.

Dirk Johnson, excerpts from "In U.S. Parks, Some Seek Retreat, But Find Crime," *The New York Times* (August 21, 1990). Copyright © 1990 by The New York Times Company. Reprinted with the permission of *The New York Times*.

Tom Ashbrook, excerpts from "A View from the East," *The Boston Globe Sunday Magazine* (February 19, 1989). Copyright © 1989 by the Globe Newspaper Company. Reprinted with the permission of *The Boston Globe*.

Phillipe Bourgois, "Just Another Night on Crack Street," *The New York Times* magazine, pages 148-150, April 20, 1987. Copyright © 1987 by The New York Times Company. Reprinted by permission.

Index

Aboulmagd, Ahmed Kamal, 104
accountability
   church leaders, 83–85
   collapse of institutional, 81–83
   corporate state, 74–75
accounting profession, and Enron scandal,
     65, 67, 68–69
Adams, Luwaunna, 94
Adelphi, 67
Adler, William, 49
affordable housing, 91
AFL-CIO, 62–63
AIDS, 13
airport deterioration, 90, 91
air rage, 8
Albert, Michael, 91
Alcoa, 59
alcoholism, on college campuses, 45
Alger, Horatio, 118
Allen, Robert, 40
Allende, Salvadore, 98
Almada, Teresa, 60
Al Qaeda
   and 9/11 attacks, 110–111
   Saddam Hussein's relation to, 106, 107,
     112
ambition, 9, 16
American Century, 35
American Dream
   among inner city drug dealers, 49–50
   and Charles Stuart, 4
   corruption of, 14–17
   and instrumental wilding, 9
   marriage as path to, 37
   media images, 40–41
   and Menendez brothers, 31, 32
   money illusion, 43–44
   and oversocialized American character,
     28
   as paean to individualistic enterprise, 7
   rethinking, 118–120
   and Rob Marshall, 22, 23, 25
   traditional high moral ideals of,
     118–119
   See also individualism
American Revolution, 119, 125
An American Tragedy (Dreiser), 33–35
anomie, 18
   and globalization, 54
   as norm, 19
anti-Americanism, 111–112
anti-Semitism, 115
antisocial behavior, 5, 8, 11, 18–19
Arbenz, Jacobo, 111

Aristotle, 114
Arrighi, Giovanni, 102, 103
Arthur Andersen, role in Enron scandal,
     68–69
Article 51, of United Nations charter,
     105–106
The Art of the Deal (Trump), 14
Ashbrook, Tom, 90
Asian financial crisis ("Asian flu"), 63
Association for the Rights of Catholics in the
     Church (ARCC), 84–85
AT&T, 40
   Grubman elevates stock rating of, 71
Austria, social market in, 120, 121
Avis, employee ownership, 123

Baltimore, David, 47
Banks, Robert, 80
banks, role in Enron scandal, 69–72
Barton, Mark, 16
Bass, Alison, 26
Bateman, Judith, 44
Batson, Neal, 70
Battle of Seattle, 61
Bechtel, post–Iraq war reconstruction
     contracts, 109
benign neglect, 121
Berardino, Joseph, 69
Berlin Wall, 114
Biggs, Barton, 71–72
Billionaire Boys' Club, 16
Bill of Rights, 85, 127
binge drinking, 45
Blair, Tony, 107
Blind Faith (miniseries), 24
Blum, Robert, 88
Bolivia, Enron energy trading, 67
Border Industrialization Program, 58
Boston archdiocese
   laity empowerment: Voice of the
     Faithful, 84
   priest sexual abuse in, 77–79
Bourgois, Philippe, 48–49
Boyer, Ernest L., 46, 47
bridge deterioration, 90–91
Britain
   Enron energy trading, 67
   protests over role in Iraq war, 107
   role in Iraq war, 104
   terrorism against in period of hegemonic
     decline, 111
   U.S. as successor to hegemonic power,
     102–103
Brown, Ron, 74

Brown, Sherrod, 58
Bruyn, Severyn, 122
Buell Elementary School shootings, 88
Buffett, Warren, 95
Bugliosi, Vincent, 101
burglary, rates of, 87
Burnett, Mark, 41
Bush, George H.W.
    Gulf War and Cheney doctrine, 108
    impact on wilding, 14
Bush, George W., 59
    attitude on unions, 23, 43, 53
    and corporate state, 72–75
    and Enron scandal, 65, 72–73
    and Harken Energy investigation, 67
    impact on wilding, 14
    Iraq war, 103–110
    promises to continue Reagan revolution,
        14, 93
    redefines self-defense after 9/11, 105
    Roadmap for Peace, 113
    small town upbringing, 119
    tax cut plans, 92, 94–95
    Texas prison building under, 99
    war on terrorism, 110–113

cafeteria-style government, 96–97
California, and Enron's fraudulent energy
        trading, 67, 73
Callahan, David, 15
campuses, See college campuses
canon law, 82, 85
capital flight, 55
capitalism
    and community, 53–55
    crisis of legitimacy after Enron, 81
    inner-city drug dealers, 49–50
    and myth of self-made man, 118
    profit versus economic wilding, 52–53
    and wilding, 12, 17–20
careerism, 9, 16
Carlson, Tucker, 99
Carnegie, Andrew, 52
cash nexus, 18, 55
casino capitalism, 103
Catholic church, wilding by priests and
        leaders, 76–85
Cendant, 67
Central America, sweatshops in, 57–58
Central Park jogger incident (1989), 2–3
Central Park Puerto Rican Day incident
        (2000), 1–2
Chambers brothers, 49–50
charitable donations, 13, 117
    possible effect of estate tax repeal, 95
cheating, 9, 10, 38–39
    on college campuses, 45, 46–47
Cheating 101 (Moore), 46–47
Cheney, Dick, 107, 109
    1990 strategy document, 108
    and Enron scandal, 67, 73
    and Halliburton investigation, 67, 68
Chentex plant, 57–58, 59
Chewko, 66, 69

child labor, 55, 63
    El Salvadorian sweatshops, 57
children
    abuse by priests, 76–85
    health insurance problems of, 91
    urgency of addressing problems of,
        124–125
    violence by, 87–90
Children's Defense Fund, 125
China, sweatshops in, 57
Chinese wall, 72
church, wilding by priests and leaders, 76–85
CIA coups, 98, 111
Citigroup, 54
    and Enron scandal, 69, 70, 71, 72
civic participation, 130
civil society
    as antidote to wilding, 114–117
    politics of, 125–127
Clark, Ramsey, 106
class divisions, 16, 20
    and prison-industrial complex, 100
clergy sexual abuse, 76–85
Clinton, Bill, 42
    Enron's relationship with Ron Brown, 74
    impact on wilding, 14
    Rich pardon, 10
    small town upbringing, 119
    support for unions and labor rights, 62
    tax cuts, 93–94
Clintonomics, 43
co-determination, 122
Cold War, 103
    as hegemonic wilding, 111
collectivism, 115
    See also communitarianism
college admission essay fraud, 46
college campuses, 44–48
    antisweatshop movement, 56–57, 64,
        130–131
colonialism, 102–103
Columbine High School shootings, 88
Combs, James, 118
commodity traders, 15–16
common good, 118, 129
communication node deterioration, 90
communism, rationale for political wilding
        during Cold War, 111
communitarianism
    and rethinking of American Dream,
        118–120
    wilding based on, 12
community, 12
    and capitalism, 53–55
    crisis in, due to individualism, 18
    multinationals as virtual, 54
    rebuilding after fall of communism, 115
    reviving moral dream of, 120
    weakness in contributes to wilding, 19
community credit unions, 122
compassionate conservatism, 92
competitiveness, 9, 10, 11
    among college students, 45
computers, as aid to college cheating, 46

Conference of Catholic Bishops, 81
Conger, Darva, 41
Constitution, of the United States, 126
Constitutional Moment, Seattle protests as, 61
contract jobs, 54
Contract with America, 93
cooperatives, 122, 123, 124
    Mondragon, 126
corpocracy, 53
corporate self-interest, 12
corporate social charters, 122
corporate state
    and collapse of institutional
        accountability, 81
    and Enron scandal, 72–75
corporate welfare, 98
corporate wilding, 12, 51–53
    after Battle of Seattle, 61–64
    and capitalism vs. community, 53–55
    Enron case, 65–75
    musical chairs game, 55–56
    Third World as global sweatshop, 56–60
Corzine, Jon, 94
Cover, Ashanna, 1
crack dealing, 48–49
Crash of 1929, Glass-Stegall Act passed
        after, 72
creative accounting, 67
credit-card debt, 43
Credit Suisse First Boston, 71
credit unions, 122
crime
    and anomie, 18
    on college campuses, 46–47
    as disparity between goals and means, 20
    and individualism, 12
    rate peak in 1990s, 87
    See also specific types of crime and
        criminals; violence
cynicism, among college students, 44–45, 47

Daily, Thomas, 80
Daschle, Tom, 94–95
Davis, Angela, 100
Davis, Yaneira, 1
day trading, 15, 16
Dean, John, 106
Dean, Shavan, 87
death (estate) tax, 95
death penalty, 99–100
De Beers, 51–52
Declaration of Independence, 85
De Genero, Ralph, 96
democracy, 118–119, 129
Democrats, new, 14
Denmark, social market in, 120
derivatives, 15–16
de Tocqueville, Alexis, 16–17, 115–116, 130
diamond industry, 51–52
Diaz, Oscar Chavez, 59
dies irae (day of rage), 8
DiIulio, John J., Jr., 95
Dingell, John, 47
disenfranchisement, of African-Americans, 101

dividend tax, 94
domestic violence, 8, 130
dot-com economy, 42–44, 67
    and corrupted American Dream, 15–16
downsizing, reality TV as mirror of, 40
Dream, See American Dream
Dreiser, Theodore, 33–35
drug dealing, 16, 48–49
    sentence disparities for crack vs. powder
        cocaine, 100
Duncan, David, 68
Dupre, Thomas L., 82
Durkheim, Émile, 17–20, 27, 54, 55, 77

Eastern Europe, 114–115
Ebbers, Bernie, 71
ecological morality, 119
economic boom of 1990s, 42–44
economic status, See poverty
economic wilding, 12
    defined, 10
    global, 56
    profit versus economic wilding, 52–53
    See also corporate wilding
education, 91, 112
    George W. Bush's proposal, 95
    government's role in, 126
    See also schools
egalitarianism, 120
egoism, 18
    and globalization, 54
    as norm, 19
Elizondo, Gustavo, 60
El Salvador, sweatshops in, 57
Emerson, Ralph Waldo, 86
empathy, 9
employee stock ownership plans (ESOPs),
        122, 123, 124
Enron scandal, 65–75, 76
    and collapse of institutional
        accountability, 81
environmental abuses
    and corporate tax subsidies, 96
    maquiladora plants, 60
equality, 118–119
estate tax, 95
ethnic cleansing, 12, 98, 115
Europe
    crime rates lower than U.S., 88
    death penalty outlawed in every nation,
        99–100
    life expectancy and infant mortality vs.
        United States, 91
    national health care, 126
    preservation of social infrastructure, 92
    social contract, 125
    social market in, 120–121, 122
European Social Charter, 63
evil behavior, and individualism, 12
export processing zones, 58
expressive wilding, 8, 9
    and anomie, 18
    and individualism, 12
externalities, 122

401K retirement plans, 123
Fair Labor Association, 64
fair play, 120
Falk, Richard, 105
family, domestic violence, 8, 130
Fastow, Andrew, 66, 69, 70
Fenrich, Ronald, 87
Fernandez-Kelly, Maria, 60
financial markets, 53–54
Findlay, Tom, 36–37
Fitzgerald, Peter, 70
Florida 2000 Presidential election count, 101
Foley, James D., 80
Ford, Charles, 26
Ford, Gregory, 78
Foster, Gina, 38
Fox, James Alan, 26, 27
France, disagreement with Iraq war, 105–106
free-market fundamentalism, 96
Free Trade Agreement of the Americas, 53
Free Trade for Africa agreement, 53
free-trade treaties, 53
free-trade zones, 58
Friedman, Milton, 19

Galligan, Thomas B., 2–3
Galston, William A., 105
Gates, Bill, 42, 119–120
Gates, William H., Sr., 95
General Electric (GE), 54
    in Mexico, 58
General Motors (GM), 54, 56
    in Mexico, 58
Generation X, 15
Genn, Coleman, 39
genocidal warfare, 12
Geoghan, John J., 78, 80
Gephardt, Richard, 94
Germany
    disagreement with Iraq war, 105–106
    national health care, 126
    social market in, 120–121, 122
Giesecke, Helmut, 120
Gifford, Kathie Lee, 57
Gilded Age, 15
Gillette, Chester, 33, 35, 36
Gingrich, Newt, 36
    attacks on government, 95
    Contract with America, 93
    social program dismantling, 14, 43
Gitlin, Anna, 38
Glass-Stegall Act, 72
Global Crossing, 67, 69
global economic wilding, 56
global economy, 53
globalization, 53–55
    after Battle of Seattle, 61–64
    musical chairs game, 55–56
    and terrorism, 113
global musical chairs, 55–56
global warming, 119
Gordon, Suzanne, 97
Gore, Albert, 74, 101

governmental wilding, 12, 52, 53
government regulation, 55–56
Gramm, Phil, 73
Gramm, Wendy, 73
Gramsci, Antonio, 102–103
Great Britain, See Britain
Great Depression, 17, 35, 119
Great Society, 120
greed, 9, 17
    new ethos of, 15
    polarization as a result of, 120
Greenwich NatWest, 69
Griffiths, Clyde, 33
Grubman, Jack, 71
Gulf War, 108

Halliburton, 67, 68
    post–Iraq war reconstruction contracts,
        109
Hamas, 113
Harken Energy, 67
Hart, Peter, 123
Hatch, Richard, 40–41
hate crimes, on college campuses, 45
Havel, Vaclav, 115
health care, 91, 112
    government's role in, 126
health insurance, 91
hegemonic decline, 103, 111
hegemony, 102
Henkin, Louis, 127
Henson, Shirley, 38
Herbert, Bob, 52
Hernandez, Michele, 46
Hiemstra, Hal, 129
highway deterioration, 90, 91
highway overpasses, heaving rocks off, 8
Hillel, 11
hockey dad killing, 38
homeless people, 91
Homestead Steel Strike, 52–53
hunger, 130
hurtful behavior, 11–12
Hussein, Saddam, 103–104, 106, 107, 108,
    112
Hussman, Lawrence, 33, 35

Ik society, 8, 18, 114
    described, 5–7
    and reality TV, 41
    as sociopathic society, 27
Imclone, 67
incipient wilding, 10
independent contractors, See contract jobs
India
    considers pre-emptive attack against
        Pakistan, 106
    Enron energy trading, 67
indifference to others, 9
individualism
    changes in past and present notions of,
        14–17
    de Tocqueville on, 17, 115–116

Durkheim and Marx on, 17–20
and myth of self-made man, 118
varieties of, 11–12
wilding as degraded form of, 10–11
See also American Dream
individualistic behaviors, 11
individualistic culture, 10–11
individual rights, 10
infant mortality, 91
information economy, 42
infrastructure deterioration, 90–92
insider trading, 16
institutional accountability, 81–83
institutional wilding, 12, 52
   Marx's view, 19–20
   See also corporate wilding
instrumental wilding, 8–9
   and anomie, 18
   institutional, 12
International Labor Organization, 63, 127
International Monetary Fund (IMF), 61, 63
intimidation, of communities by capital
         flight, 55
Iraq war, 102, 103–110
Israel-Palestine conflict, 113

Jackson, Derrick, 101
Japan
   crime rates lower than U.S., 88
   individualization cushioned by culture,
      19
   social contract, 125–126
Jefferson, Thomas, 85
Jimmy Fund theft, 46
Jordan, Michael, 118
Josephson, Michael, 89
J.P. Morgan Chase, and Enron scandal, 69,
      70
judicial partisanship, 101
Jumaa, Qabil Khazzal, 104
The Jungle (Sinclair), 57
junk bonds, 15

Kader Industrial Toy Company, 52
Kanter, Donald, 44
Kelly, Kevin, 23–24
Kennedy, Donald, 47
Kernaghan, Charles, 57
King, Ralph, 28
King, Rodney, 99
Kmart, 67
Koch, Edward, 3
Kukdong factory, 58–59
Kuttner, Robert, 96
Kuwait, 108

labor unions, *See* unions
laity, of Catholic Church
   and accountability of priests for sexual
         abuse, 76, 81–83
   empowerment of, 83–85
Lancelot, Jill, 96
land trusts, 122–123

Lane, Deidre, 21
Las Mercedes Free-Trade Zone, 57
Law, Bernard, 76, 79–81
Lawrence, Josina, 1
Lay, Kenneth, 66, 71, 72–73
layoffs, *See* downsizing
Lebed, Jonathan, 15
Leeson, Nicholas, 15
legal profession, and Enron scandal, 65
Levin, Jack, 26, 27
Lieberman, Joseph, 74
life expectancy, 91
LJM 2, 66, 70
LJM Cayman, 66
Long, Russell, 124
love, 114, 115
Lowry, Ritchie, 123
Lunsford, Frederic Welborn, 21
lying, 9, 10

MacLeish, Roderick, 78
manipulation, in reality TV, 40–41
maquiladora plants, 58–60
   unionization efforts, 59, 62–63
marangik (Ik concept of goodness), 7
market bubble of 1990s, 67
   role of Wall Street analysts' conflicts of
      interest, 71–72
market system, 11
marriage, as path to American Dream, 37
Marshall, Chris, 22
Marshall, Maria, 22–26
Marshall, Robert Oakley, 22–26, 27–28, 34
Marshall, Roby, 22
Martha Stewart Enterprises, 67
Martin, Joseph, 47–48
Marx, Karl, 17–19, 54–55
materialism, 35
   accepting limits on, 119–120
Matsui, Robert T., 91
McGinniss, Joe, 23
McKinney, Cynthia, 58
McSorley, Patrick, 78
McVeigh, Timothy J., 95, 96
Mead, Margaret, 1, 6
Menendez brothers (Eric and Lyle), 28–33,
      34
Menendez, José, 28–29, 30
Menendez, Kitty, 28, 29
Merrill Lynch, role in Enron scandal, 69–72
Merton, Robert, 20
Mesa, Joseph M., Jr., 46
Mexico, *maquiladora* plants, 58–60, 62–63
middle class, 16
   new constraints on, 44
   view of wilding, 3
military spending, 102
militia movement, 95–96
Milken, Michael, 10
Mills, C. Wright, 22
Milosevic, Slobodan, 98
Mirvis, Philip, 44
misdemeanors, 9

The Mole, 40, 41
Mondragon cooperative, 126
money illusion, 43–44
Montagu, Ashley, 7
Moore, Michael, 46–47
moral compass, 13, 18
morality, 114, 115, 118
moral restraint, 9, 86
Morganthau, Hans, 102
Morris, Erik, 87
Mossadegh, Mohammed, 111
mountain people, *See* Ik society
Mullin, Jay, 80
multinational firms, 52, 53
    as virtual community, 54
murder
    rates of, 87
    ultimate wilders: killing family for
        money, 4, 8, 21–37
    See also violence
Murrah Federal Building bombing, 95–96

9/11 World Trade Tower attacks, 105,
        110–111
Nader, Ralph, 98
NAFTA, *See* North American Free Trade
        Agreement
narcissistic personality disorder, 27
New Deal, 17, 55, 120
new economy, *See* dot-com economy
Nicaragua, sweatshops in, 57–58
Niger, Iraq's alleged attempt to buy uranium
        from, 106–107
Nike
    and Fair Labor Association, 63–64
    in Mexico, 58, 59
No Cares Cohort, 97
North American Free Trade Agreement
        (NAFTA), 53, 58
    environmental and labor agreements,
        63

oil interests
    and Gulf Wars, 108, 109
    rationale for political wilding during
        Cold War, 111
Oklahoma City bombing, 95–96
O'Neill, Paul, 59, 109
oversocialization, 19, 26–28
Oziel, L. Jerome, 30

Pakistan, India considers preemptive attack
        against, 106
Palestine-Israel conflict, 113
parochial schools, 91
patriot militias, 95–96
pedophilia, priests, 77–79
people's capitalism, 124
Perle, Richard, 109
petty wilding, 9–10
Phillips, Kevin, 43
physical infrastructure deterioration, 90–92
pinprick attacks, in New York City, 87

Pitt, Harvey, 72, 73
Plachy, Joann, 46
plagiarism, 46–47
police, unorthodox tactics in Central Park
        jogger case, 3
police brutality, 98–99
political citizenship, 126
political corruption, 17
political rights, 126
political wilding, 92–98
    defined, 10
    and state-sponsored violence, 98–101
politics of secession, 16, 128, 129
Pope Paul VI, 85
Populorum Progressio (Pope Paul VI), 85
port deterioration, 90
Poussaint, Alvin, 4
poverty, 92
    appetites-opportunities gap, 43–44
    and corruption of American Dream, 16
    Mexican *maquiladora* workers, 60
    and prison-industrial complex, 100
    and social infrastructure deterioration, 91
    U.S. rate triple Europe's, 43
Powers, John, 96–97
predatory business practices, 52
    and globalization, 54
pre-emptive self-defense, as motivation for
        Iraq war, 105
priest sexual abuse, 76–85
prison-industrial complex, 100–101
prison labor, 55, 63, 100
profiteering, 12
Progressive Era, 17
Project Bread, 116
public-policy wilding, 92–93
public schools, 91
Putin, Vladimir, 106

Qwest, 67

racial attacks, on college campuses, 45
racial profiling, 100
racism
    and prison-industrial complex, 100
    and Stuart murder, 4
railway deterioration, 90
rape
    Central Park jogger incident (1989), 2–3
    on college campuses, 45
    by priests, 77–79
Raptor, 66, 69
Reagan, Ronald, 42
    attacks on government, 95
    attacks unions, 43, 53
    impact on wilding, 14
    social market innovations, 124
Reaganomics, 43
Reagan revolution, 14, 19, 93
reality TV, 40–41
Reebok, and Fair Labor Association, 63–64
Rehnquist, Chief Justice William, 127
Reich, Robert, 16, 128

research fraud, 47
Reyes, Matias, 3
Rich, Marc, 10
Richardson, Kevin, 2
Rivers, Chirll, 89
road deterioration, 90, 91
Roadmap for Peace, 113
road rage, 8, 38
Roaring Twenties, 17, 53
robber barons, 14, 17, 34, 52–53
Robertson, Pat, 95
Robin Hood Foundation, 117
Rockefeller, John D., 52
Rockwell, Rick, 41
Rolland, Kayla, 88
Rome, terrorism against in period of
    hegemonic decline, 111
Roosevelt, Franklin Delano, 119
    and Glass-Stegall Act, 72
Rosenbaum, Ruth, 59
Rove, Karl, 110
Rumsfeld, Donald, 109
Russia, disagreement with Iraq war, 106
Ryan, George, 99–100

St. Valentine's Day Massacre (bankruptcy
    report on Enron scandal), 70
Salman, Talal, 104
Salomon Smith Barney, 71
Salvucci, Frederick P., 91
Sandifer, Robert, 87
savings-and-loan crooks, 9
Savoy, Paul, 127
Scahill, James J., 82, 83
school board corruption, 39
schools
    infrastructure deterioration, 91
    violence in, 8, 88–89
Schultz, George, 109
Schumer, Charles, 74
science fraud, 47
Seattle, WTO protests (Battle of Seattle), 61
Second Vatican Council, 84
Securities and Exchange Commission (SEC),
    73–74
self-help groups, 130
self-interest, 19
    Catholic Church, 83
    cooperation for common good as
      enlightened form of, 129
    and degraded individualism, 11
    de Tocqueville on, 116
    states, 102
self-made man, 118
sewer system deterioration, 90
sexual abuse, by priests, 76–85
sexual harassment
    in *maquiladoras*, 59–60
    in sweatshops, 51
Shames, Laurence, 15
Shanley, Paul, 78, 80
Shannon, John, 129
shareholders, 81

Short, Claire, 107
Sierra Leone war, 51–52
Simpson, O. J., 8–9
Sinclair, Upton, 57
Skilling, Jeffrey, 66, 69
small towns, community as American
    mythology, 119
Smart, Pamela, 21–22, 26, 27–28, 34
Smith, Adam, 19
Smith, Susan, 36–37
social accounting, 123
social activism, 13
social capital, 123
social citizenship, 126
social contract, 125–126
social fabric, 91
    wilding's effect on, 8, 10
social infrastructure
    deterioration of, 90, 91–92
    repairing, 128–129
    and tax cuts, 96
social investing, 123
socialization
    and individualism, 18
    oversocialization, 19, 26–28
    undersocialization, 18
social market, 120–125
social movements, 130–131
social obligations, 127
social reconstruction, 117–118
social rights, 125–126, 127
social screens, 123
social services, 91
    government's role in, 126
social solidarity, 18
social wilding
    defined, 10
    grandiose dreams and restricted
      opportunities make recipe for, 16
socioeconomic status, *See* poverty
sociology, 18
sociopathic society, 27
sociopathy
    of elites, 13–14
    and oversocialization, 26–28
    ultimate wilders, 26–28
Soros, George, 95
Soviet Union, 103, 111, 114
sports rage, 8, 38
state-sponsored violence, 98–101, 102
states' rights movement, 93
Steffens, Lincoln, 34
steroid use, 12
stock market, *See* Wall Street
Stone, Robert, 28–29
Stuart, Carol, 4
Stuart, Charles, 8, 22, 26, 27–28, 34, 35, 36
    murder of wife, 4
suburbs
    mean-spirited image, 97–98
    and politics of secession, 128, 129
suicide, and anomie, 18
Sullivan, Jimmy, 39

Supreme Court, 101
Survivor, 40–41
Survivor II: The Australian Outback, 40–41
sweatshops, 51–52, 130–131
    Third World as global sweatshop, 56–60
Sweden
    individualization cushioned by culture,
       19
    social market in, 120, 121
Sweeney, Constance M., 80, 81
Sweeney, John, 62
systemic wilding
    and corporate state, 74–75
    defined, 65–66
    Enron, 65–75
    priest sexual abuse, 76–85

Tate, Lionel, 87
tax cuts, 92–98, 112
tax revolt, 93, 117
Taylor, John, 15
Teapot Dome scandal, 17
Tejada, Charles J., 3
television, 40–41
temporary workers, 54
Temptation Island, 40, 41
terrorism
    war on terrorism, 102, 110–113
    World Trade Tower attacks on
       9/11/2001, 105, 110–111
Texas justice system, 99, 100
textile industry, move from Northern to
       Southern cities to avoid unions,
       55
Thailand toy factory fire, 52
theft, on college campuses, 45
Third Wave revolution, 93
Third World, as global sweatshop, 56–60
Thoreau, Henry David, 21, 34
Tilney, Elizabeth, 70
Tilney, Schuyler, 70
To Die For, 22
Toffler, Alvin and Heidi, 93
tolerance, 118–119
Trausch, Susan, 38–39
Triangle Shirtwaist factory fire, 52
trickle-up tax policies, 98
Trump, Donald, 3, 14–15
trust, 114, 115
Tucker, Karla Faye, 99
Turnbull, Colin, 5–7, 8
Twain, Mark, 34
Tyco, 67

unions
    demonization of, 42, 53
    maquiladora unionization efforts, 59,
       62–63
    resurrection of, 130–131
    textile mills, 55
United Airlines, employee ownership, 123
United Nations, disagreement with Iraq war,
       105–106

United Nations Universal Declaration on
       Human Rights, 84, 85, 127
United States
    anti-Americanism and war on terrorism,
       111–112
    as successor to Britain's hegemonic
       power, 102–103
    See also American Dream
upper class, 16
    under Reaganomics, 43
U.S. Conference of Catholic Bishops, 81

violence, 17
    domestic, 8, 130
    and individualism, 12
    and oversocialization, 26–28
    state-sponsored, 98–101, 102
    in streets, 86–89
Voice of the Faithful, 84
volunteer work, 13, 130

Waco tragedy, 100
wages, 42–43
wag the dog strategy, 110
Walk for Hunger, 116
Wallerstein, Immanuel, 102
Wall Street
    and corrupted American Dream, 15–16
    financing of global economy, 53
    market bubble of 1990s and soaring
       stock prices in, 67
    Robin Hood Foundation, 117
    role in Enron scandal, 65, 69–72
Wall Street analysts, conflict of interest,
       71–72
Wal-Mart
    annual sales, 54
    and Fair Labor Association, 63–64
war on terrorism, 102, 110–113
Watkins, Sherron, 66
wealth
    concentration in fewer hands, 42–44
    pressure to pursue, 15
    single-minded pursuit of, 9
weapons of mass destruction (WMD),
       rationale for Iraq war, 106
Weber, Max, 99, 102
Weirton Steel, employee ownership, 123
welfare, 43, 94
White, John J., 78
White, Steven, 32
White, Thomas, 73
white lies, 9
white man's burden, 102–103
Who Wants to Marry a Millionaire, 41
wilders
    new ethos rewards, 13
    and two Americas, 13–14, 117
    ultimate wilders: killing family for
       money, 4, 8, 21–37
wilding
    causes, 17–20
    civil society as antidote to, 114–115

on college campuses, 44–48
cycles of wilding periods alternating with
    civility, 17
domestic violence, 8, 130
epidemic in America, 8–10
in everyday life, 38–40
famous incidents, 1–5
forms of, 8–10
hopeful signs, 115–118
infrastructure deterioration, 90–92
Iraq war and war on terror, 102–113
legitimation, 17
and new communitarianism, 118–120
origin of term, 2–3
and social market, 120–125
stopping, 128–131
systemic wilding at Enron, 65–75
systemic wilding by church leaders and
    priests, 76–85
and tax revolt, 92–98
television's influence, 40–41
two Americas, 13–14, 117
types of, 10–11
violence in streets, 86–89
See also economic wilding; expressive
    wilding; institutional wilding;
    instrumental wilding; political
    wilding; social wilding

wilding culture, 13
wilding society, 14
Williams, Patricia, 3
Wise, Kharey, 2
Woburn, Massachusetts, toxic chemicals in,
    129
Wolfe, Alan, 115
Wolfensohn, James, 62
wolfpack, 2
worker ownership, 122–124
workplace rage, 8
World Bank, 61
WorldCom, 65, 67, 68, 69, 71
World Economic Forum, 61
world system theory, 102, 103
World Trade Association, 61, 63
World Trade Organization (WTO), 53
    and Battle of Seattle, 61–62, 63
World Trade Tower attacks on 9/11/2001,
    105, 110–111

youth
    on campuses, 44–48
    expressive wilding, 8
    See also children

Zephyrus, 70
Zionists, 111